MORE
GHOST

STORIES OF NOVA SCOTIA

VERNON OICKLE
FOREWORD BY DARRYLL WALSH

MacIntyre Purcell Publishing Inc.

MacIntyre Purcell Publishing Inc.
194 Hospital Rd.
Lunenburg, Nova Scotia
B0J 2C0
(902) 640-3350

www.macintyrepurcell.com
info@macintyrepurcell.com

Printed and bound in Canada by Friesens

Cover design: Kevin O'Reilly
Book design: Alex Hickey
Author photo (back cover): David Dobson

ISBN: 978-1-77276-132-0

Library and Archives Canada Cataloguing in Publication

Title: More ghost stories of Nova Scotia / Vernon Oickle.
Names: Oickle, Vernon, 1961- author.
Identifiers: Canadiana 20190106174 I ISBN 9781772761320 (softcover)
Subjects: LCSH: Ghosts—Nova Scotia. I LCSH: Haunted places—Nova Scotia.
Classification: LCC BF1472.C3 O426 2015 I DDC 133.109716—dc23

MacIntyre Purcell Publishing Inc. would like to acknowledge the financial support of the Government of Canada and the Nova Scotia Department of Tourism, Culture and Heritage.

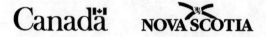

Dedicated to my good friend and fellow researcher,
Darryll Walsh

Acknowledgements

I would like to thank the following people for their help and support in making this book possible: Darryll Walsh, Chris Mills, David Pottier, and Alessandra Nadudvari, for their help in providing material and photos; Chris Benjamin for his excellent editing skills, Alex Hickey for her great design and publisher John MacIntyre for green lighting this project. I would also like to thank my wife Nancy for her excellent navigating skills and for her moral support throughout this entire process. And finally, I would like to thank all those people who shared their stories. Without you, this book would not be possible.

Foreword

Would ghosts exist if we didn't believe in them?
Fervent skeptics would have us believe a little education would extinguish such silly "superstitions." They must be perennially disappointed then to learn poll after poll records a healthy majority of adults continue to believe in the supernatural even in this well educated, technological world.

The skeptics miss the point entirely. Superstition, as an attempt to explain the unexplainable, is merely a primitive form of science. Though we have developed a marvellous system of determining truth and the operating parameters of reality within a 95 percent probability of being correct, we also need to believe in the unbelievable.

For a variety of external and internal reasons, ghosts shall always exist in our minds. We need to believe in the continuation of ourselves after death. Our culture reinforces and feeds this need. Our families pass down personal experiences generation after generation. And most importantly ... it's fun!

Some chroniclers of the supernatural have been touched personally by it, while many simply ride the economic winds that ghosts bring. To those of us who have experienced the unexplainable and write about it for a living, there is a self-imposed burden to get the story right. Not to create simply for entertainment purposes, but to understand supernatural experiences, to chronicle "true" stories, to share them in the hope they will help others do the same.

Vernon Oickle has shouldered that burden well for a couple of decades now. He does so as a journalist and as someone who has experienced something he cannot readily explain. He recognizes the value in these experiences, if only for future scholars to understand. Each volume on ghosts he has written is eminently entertaining, and this one will be no different.

I have been a parapsychologist for almost a quarter century. As a boy, I used to sit on my uncle's knee to eagerly receive our family heritage of the mysterious, and I got goosebumps. As I write this now, late on a very stormy January night, those same goosebumps return, eagerly awaiting my chance to read *More Ghost Stories of Nova Scotia*.

—Darryll Walsh, Ph.D.

From the Author

Can you feel it?

That icy tingle racing up and down your spine, doing a tap dance between your shoulder blades.

The tiny hairs on your arms that are standing at attention as if motivated by an electrical charge.

That butterfly in the pit of your stomach doing somersaults as your mouth goes dry and swallowing becomes a nearly impossible chore because you have no spit; your tongue feels like a piece of shoe leather, unable to move.

The breath catching in your throat as you try to choke back the fear.

Yes, my friend, sometimes there really is a reason to be afraid of things that go bump in the night.

As we begin this journey into the paranormal, I invite you to find a comfy chair, dim the lights, take a deep breath, steel your nerves, and enjoy these true encounters with the world from beyond what we know, the world that we consider to be normal — whatever normal is.

Remember. To truly embrace these tales from the other side, you must let go of your inhibitions, let down your defences, suspend your beliefs, shrug off the logic that destroys imagination, and open your mind to the possibility.

Most of all, you must believe that there are things that happen in this world that defy simple explanation and basic logic. Sometimes, there simply are no answers to your questions.

Between these covers are stories of the supernatural — and they are all true. I wish to thank all of those brave souls who have told me their stories so that I may share them with you. This book would not be possible without each of you and you all have my undying gratitude.

Now, dear reader, you may begin. Are you sure you are ready?

— Vernon Oickle,
Author

Table of Contents

A Personal Encounter

I have been researching, writing and telling ghost stories for at least four decades and while it is often difficult to explain some of the things I have encountered and experienced over the years, it's a subject that is near to my heart. One of the most — if not, the most — common questions I'm asked is whether I believe in ghosts. My answer is simple — I don't not believe.

I appreciate that some things defy reality and for that reason, I am committed to always keeping an open mind. Furthermore, when someone relates their personal experiences, I never judge their sincerity or their compassion. That is not my role. I am a collector, a researcher and a storyteller. I leave the final judgment to someone else, that being the reader or listener.

All of that being said, I must confess that I do believe there are things that happen in this world that we cannot easily explain. Are we so naive that we believe humans are the only intelligent inhabitants of this world? I can say without hesitation that I have seen things and I have had experiences that lead me to draw this conclusion — no, we are not!

Anyone who has encountered a ghostly being or who has had a paranormal experience will tell you, the experience was unlike anything they've previously witnessed or felt. For these people, such an encounter is confirmation that maybe, just maybe, there is something beyond the confines of our human world.

Is there life after death? No one can say for sure, but whether you choose to believe it or not, encounters with the paranormal are real. That I can tell you with 100 percent certainty because I have had several such encounters over the years, the most recent being in the summer of 2018.

Before I share my personal encounter, I will give you some backstory. I had a sister. Her name was Heather and she was two years older than me. Her birthday was August 17, 1959 and she died on September 19, 1991 of complications from leukemia. She had bravely fought the disease for two years but, sadly, sometimes, the body becomes too tired and too weak to continue fighting against the ravages of such a disease. And so I lost the only sibling I had. It was an ordeal I do not believe I will ever truly overcome.

As children, Heather and I were close. I have many fond memories from my childhood of the good times we shared camping as a family, and the times we did things that did not sit well with our parents. The infractions were nothing serious, mind you. Just the regular run-of-the mill childish mischief. As the oldest, Heather was the instigator but I was usually game to do whatever she told me to do. When we got into trouble, we shared the punishment as a duo, but that was part of the fun and those memories are as vivid today as if they happened only yesterday.

But life happens. I know that and I accept the inevitable that awaits us all. It doesn't mean I have to like it but I understand that when life throws some hardships in your direction, as it always does, you must find a way to move on and I did that. It wasn't always easy and there are times I miss Heather. It would be great to have someone to talk to, someone who shares a common history with me. Then there are times when I feel that she is still with me and that brings me to my story.

It was early on the morning of August 17, 2018 — the day that would have been Heather's 59th birthday. In fact, it was shortly after 6 a.m. and my youngest son, Colby, and I were getting ready for work. We have a normal routine that we follow every day but on this particular morning, he called me into the bathroom for some assistance because his razor wasn't working properly.

As I entered the bathroom I closed the door behind me because my wife, Nancy, was still asleep and we didn't want to disturb her. I wasn't in the bathroom but a minute when Colby and I clearly heard a woman say to us, "Hurry up. I have to pee."

The voice was loud and clear. The words were easy to distinguish.

In fact, I opened the door expecting see my wife standing there and waiting to get into the bathroom but to my surprise, there was no one there.

"Did you hear that?" I asked Colby.

"Yes," he answered, nodding his head. "Mom needs the bathroom."

Well, if she needed the bathroom so badly, where did she go?

I checked throughout the house looking for whoever had asked to use the bathroom. Eventually, I made my way to the bedroom where I found my wife sound asleep in bed.

Odd, I thought, because I was sure I had heard someone — a woman — ask to use the bathroom.

Returning to my son, I asked Colby to tell me exactly what he heard and he told me that he heard a woman say, "Hurry up. I have to pee." He then asked, "Wasn't it Mom?"

No, I told him. It was not, because his mother was still sleeping.

Now, if I had been the only one to hear the voice, I would dismiss this as me just hearing things or as me having an overactive imagination, but the fact that the two us both heard this woman say the same thing gave me reason to pause. If it wasn't Nancy asking to get into the bathroom, then who was it?

I had no idea. In fact, I still have no idea who the voice belonged to.

Perhaps it was because this happened on my sister's birthday, but the more I thought about what Colby and I heard that morning, the more I began thinking about Heather. Eventually, I recalled that when she and I were children, she had developed this terrible habit of always wanting to get into the bathroom just as soon as someone else got in there.

We only had one bathroom in our house and it didn't matter who was in there, a member of the family or a visitor to our home, Heather was always asking them to hurry up as she needed to use the facilities. And then it hit me and her words rushed back. As clear as day, I could remember her saying, "Hurry up. I have to pee."

Now, some will say this was a mere coincidence or that my mind was playing tricks on me that morning.

Really? Then how do you explain that my son and I heard the exact same thing at the exact same time? As well, was it a coincidence that this incident occurred on August 17, Heather's birthday or was it something else? Was she reaching out to me? Was she letting me know that she was with me that day?

I have no answers and there are no simple explanations for what happened that morning. To anyone who believes in the paranormal, however, the answer is straightforward. And for me, someone who has studied the paranormal, this experience was further proof that sometimes, there really is no simple explanation.

Sometimes, you just have to suspend belief and that, my friends, is exactly what I am asking you to do as we embark on this journey.

The Haunting of Catherine McIntosh

Catherine McIntosh
Daughter of Robert McIntosh
Died April 23rd, 1889
Aged 8 Y'rs & 11 Mo's

Suffer Little Children and
Forbid them not to come
Unto Me for of such is the
Kingdom of Heaven.

The above inscription is carved into a headstone that marks the grave of a young Pictou County girl who died way too young, before her ninth birthday. There are many mysteries that surround this little girl and that of her final resting place.

For starters, how did she die and why is her grave located in an isolated piece of forest about a kilometre from the actual cemetery, far from the nearest settlement?

Not much is known about the young girl, but Catherine McIntosh's grave can be found on the Greenvale Road at a place known as Thorburn Exchange in Pictou County. According to local legend, the young girl succumbed to some mysterious childhood disease and was actually buried near the family farm, as her parents could not bear to be away from her.

Today, though, any signs of a house or any other buildings are long gone, having rotted into the annals of history.

In time, the forest grew up around the child's final resting place. Today her headstone is the only physical reminder of her existence. Besides that, all that remains are the many local legends surrounding the girl and her grave.

Photo by Warren Robert

The lonely grave of Catherine McIntosh on the Greenvale Road in Thorburn Exchange in Pictou County.

Now, perhaps because of the mysterious circumstances of her death and burial, the girl's gravesite is reputed to be visited by her spirit. Stories of the haunted gravesite have gained momentum over the years, spreading across the countryside. The location is one of the most popular haunted sites in Pictou County, if not all of Nova Scotia.

To find Catherine's grave it is necessary to drive past the Cross Roads Country Market in Thorburn Exchange and onward until you come to a dirt road. Take that road and drive for another seven to eight kilometres until you see the grave on the right-hand side of the road. It's just there, all by itself, tucked away under the trees and bushes.

While over the years there have been few reports of anyone actually seeing anything at the gravesite, there have been countless reports of people "feeling" things and "sensing" things. Many people have also insisted they "heard" things while at the gravesite.

Other reports suggest that Catherine actually plays with the many toys that visitors leave at her grave. Some witnesses have said they have seen tiny handprints in the dust on the vehicles, the dust having been picked up during the drive over the dirt road. Other reports claim that small, child-sized footprints have been seen in the mud or snow around the gravesite.

And then there are the giggles that many have said they've heard while visiting the grave. Some have said that whatever is at the location has been known to grab or touch people. Whatever is at the gravesite of this little girl, there is a general agreement that it is not violent.

Truro resident and paranormal investigator Earle Lattie has visited Catherine's gravesite three times and during each of those visits he says his experiences convinced him that there is, indeed, something going on at that location that defies any logical explanation.

"I don't know what's there, what it is," he says, recalling his visits, "but a spirit or something has left an energy at that place."

It is odd, Earle agrees, pointing out that during his visit he didn't actually see anything, but he could *feel* something, as if it was embracing him.

"There is no denying that something of a paranormal nature is going on at that location," he insists. "The whole while I was there, I could not shake the feeling that something was watching me. It just made me feel uncomfortable."

Additionally, he points out, the EMF (electromagnetic field) readings were off the charts. He is convinced that some type of presence is tethered to the little girl's grave.

Warren Robert, Earle's friend and another paranormal investigator, agrees with his colleague's conclusion.

Visitors to the grave of young Catherine McIntosh leave toys for the child's spirit.

"This was a place I had always wanted to visit because I had heard so much about the Catherine McIntosh grave," Warren begins. "And I could tell right away when I finally got there, that there was something oddly special about the place; it was more than a little strange."

The moment he stepped out of his vehicle, Warren says of the day he visited, he could feel the energy. It was strong and he recalls that it kind of enveloped him and his companion.

"We stayed for a bit and during the whole time we were there, I could not shake the feeling that something was watching us and trying to get our attention," he says.

However, he quickly adds, they never once felt any type of malice toward them.

"Whatever is there doesn't mean to do anyone any harm," Warren observes. "But I have been to a lot of places that are supposed to be haunted or have some type of paranormal energy connected to it, but I have never felt anything like what I felt at that gravesite."

Something is there, both Earle and Warren insist, but what? There are more questions than answers surrounding Catherine McIntosh, but one fact remains: her story is left untold.

Ole Duke

It has been a tough year. Ever since Albert died after a courageous battle with prostate cancer, both Martha and Ole Duke — the man's faithful four-legged companion of almost 17 years — have struggled to go on with their lives.

Somehow Martha, Albert's devoted wife of 47 years, has managed to accept that her beloved husband is gone. Although it has been a struggle at times for the Truro-area woman, she has managed to pick up the pieces and put her life back together. She worries about Ole Duke though. It seems to her that the mixed-breed mutt has not been able to deal with his grief. Instead he has spent the last year moping around the house. He pines for his deceased master, the man who raised him from a pup and with whom he spent most of his life.

"Come on Duke," Martha says, placing a bowl of fresh water in front of him as he lies near the back door bathed in the late afternoon sunshine spilling in through the small window.

It's as if the dog is waiting for Albert to walk through the door and greet him, just like he did so many times throughout the years, starting when Duke was just a puppy. They originally got the dog for the children, but it quickly became evident that the real bond existed between man and dog. Soon, the two were inseparable.

"You've got to pull yourself together," she whispers, rubbing her wrinkled, arthritic fingers through the dog's coarse, brown fur that's now sporting patches of white, some becoming more prominent in recent months.

"I know you miss him. I miss him too," she says, looking into the dog's huge, dopey brown eyes where she sees nothing but sadness and loneliness. "Very much. But Albert's been gone for a year now and as much as it pains me to tell you this, he is not coming back. If you don't eat or drink something, you'll get sick and Albert wouldn't want you to make yourself sick. He wouldn't want you to give up."

The dog's eyebrows rise and fall as if the animal understands the words the elderly and kind woman is saying. He likes her, but she's no Albert.

"Listen Duke, I promised Albert I would take care of you after he was gone," Martha continues with a deep sigh. "But you haven't made it easy for me," she adds, as a sudden and cold breeze rushes through the kitchen, causing her to shiver.

"Odd," she thinks, grabbing hold of the doorknob and pulling herself back up onto her wobbly legs. She's certain there are no windows open in the house so she has no idea where the draft could have originated. It may be August and the air may be hot outside, but she still finds it cold and having the windows open is too much for her.

Glancing around the kitchen, she says to the dog that also has managed to pull itself back up to its four legs, "Did you feel that too?"

The dog whines, looks confusedly at her, but remains still.

"Come on Duke," she whispers, slowly moving around the wooden table and through the kitchen that was decorated almost 50 years earlier after she and

Albert purchased the modest three-bedroom two-level home in this community where they were both born and spent their entire lives. "Come with me."

Albert had promised her for years that he would someday buy her a grand house with four bedrooms, two bathrooms and a fancy kitchen with all the modern appliances. On the wages he earned, there was no way he could afford to honour those promises, but she had no problems with that. She knew what she was getting when she said yes to his marriage proposal and despite some tough times, he managed to provide her and their three children with a comfortable home.

The family was never hungry and they were always warm in winter, but Martha will admit there were times, when they had to struggle to make ends meet, that she wished things were different. Those thoughts were few and far between, though. All that mattered to her was that they were together and her family was healthy.

She was devastated when Albert died and now, in the twilight of her own life, she has come to understand that it's not the material things that matter. What matters to her is knowing that they did the best they could, that they nurtured their two daughters and one son into wonderful adults, that they loved and cared for one another and helped others in their community when they needed a hand.

By no means would she consider herself or Albert to be saints, but she takes comfort in knowing that they lived clean lives and she's happy for the time they had together.

When Albert got sick a few years ago, she thought her world would end if he died and when it finally happened a year ago today, that's exactly how she felt. However, in time, she came to understand that her only alternative was to pick up the pieces and move on, or else she too would face certain demise. While she misses him dearly, she isn't ready to pack it in just yet. She believes she's still got a lot of living left to do and she is determined to make the most of it.

"I have no idea where that draft came from," she says to the dog, which is slowly shuffling along behind her as she moves through the living room. It's become like a shrine to her family, with pictures of her children and grandchildren covering most exposed surfaces, including the walls, several shelving units, tables and the top of the television. She has seven grandchildren and she loves every one of them, so she keeps their images prominently displayed as a reminder of the lives she and Albert shared.

"Let's see if we can find it and put an end to it," she tells her furry companion.

Quietly, the dog makes its way to the bottom of the stairs, flops on its hind haunches and stares up to the second level.

"Up there, Duke?" Martha says, reaching the bottom of the stairs. "You think the draft came from upstairs? I've never felt it before so where could it be coming from now?"

Turning to the dog that is watching her every move, she asks, "Are you coming up with me?"

Instead of following the woman, the dog drops to the floor and buries its nose under its front paws. It whines softly and rolls its big, brown eyes, but shows little sign of life.

"Suit yourself, you lazy thing," she smiles as she starts to slowly climb the stairs. She remembers a time when the dog would sprint up the stairs in front of her and be at the top landing before she cleared the second step. "You know," she adds, turning to face Duke, "A little exercise might do you some good."

The dog rolls its eyes in her direction again, but holds its ground.

"Okay then," she shrugs. "If that's your final decision. I won't be long."

Despite an exhaustive search of the upstairs, Martha cannot find an open window — not that she expected to — nor can she locate the source of the draft. She has no idea where else to look, but she will make a mental note to talk to her son about it the next time he drops by to check on things. Maybe he can find it, she thinks.

"So Duke," she says, descending the stairs minutes later. "Looks like the draft remains a mystery."

The dog whines and opens its eyes.

"So what now?" she asks, glancing at the clock on the living room wall. "Will you look at the time, Duke? Looks like I should get us some supper. What would you like today? I'm going to have the rest of that barley soup that's in the fridge. May as well clean that up. And what about you?"

She pauses as if waiting for the dog to answer.

"I know," she finally grins. "I think there's a bit of that roast left from last weekend when the kids were over for supper. How about I warm that up for you and you can clean off the bone? That sounds good, doesn't it? You always did like my roasts."

She looks at the dog. It doesn't respond.

"I'll take that as a yes," Martha smiles at Duke, then turns and heads back toward the kitchen when she's stopped short by a sudden and loud series of bangs that ring throughout the house.

"Oh my," she reacts, her breath catching in her throat.

"What was that, Duke?" she says, backing up to where the dog has risen to its four legs.

"That sounded like doors slamming shut, didn't it?" She glances down at her furry companion. Duke has returned to the bottom of the staircase.

"Is that what it sounded like to you?"

The dog glances up at her and blinks.

"Okay, Duke," Martha whispers. "I don't know what's going on here, but I am starting to get a little scared. I don't like this so I'm going to phone Tommy. Maybe we should have him come over right away and look around for us just to be safe."

The dog whines.

"You think that's a good idea?" she continues, moving to a small corner table in the living room where the phone is stationed.

"If you were any kind of watch dog you'd go check things out for me," she chuckles, picking up the phone and starting to dial her son's number.

The dog whines again.

"I'm just kidding, Duke," Martha says, feeling bad that she may have insulted her companion. "I know you're a good dog. You're just tired, that's all. Tommy won't mind coming over."

"Seven," she whispers dialing the second to last digit of her son's number when a crash, followed by shattering glass, gives her a start.

"Oh my," she reacts, dropping the phone.

"What in the world?"

Spinning around she sees that a framed picture of Albert that had been hanging near the kitchen door has fallen to the floor and the glass has smashed. The picture that showed Albert standing beside an 18-point-buck — the largest deer he ever shot in his lifetime of hunting — was one of her husband's fondest possessions. He was only 37 when the picture was taken, but he insisted that it be displayed throughout the years for all to see. It has been hanging in that exact location for many, many years and she can't understand why it would fall off the wall today ... of all days.

She didn't like the picture much, but she agreed to hang it on the wall because she knew it gave Albert so much pleasure. She also knew it gave him the opportunity to tell anyone who would listen about his hunting excursions. He figured anyone who asked about the picture must be interested in hunting so he took that as an invitation to ramble on about his great exploits.

She didn't have the heart to tell him that most people really didn't give a flying fig about such things. Instead, they only asked him about the picture to be polite or maybe as a way to kick start a conversation. She's sure he bored many of their guests over the years with his stories, but she never told him the difference. If it made him happy to talk about hunting, then she let him have those moments. As for those who were forced to listen, she usually ended up apologizing to them before they left.

"Albert?" Martha whispers softly, moving toward the shattered glass and broken wooden frame that are now in a heap on the floor below the place it had hanged for many years.

"Are you here?" she asks, staring down at her husband's image, his youthful face grinning back up at her from the faded colour picture. "What do you want?"

She pauses, then asks, "Are you trying to tell me something?"

Grabbing hold of a nearby armchair, she slowly lowers her body and kneels on the floor in front of the mess.

"Why have you come back?" she asks, carefully reaching through the shards of broken glass and grabbing a corner of the photograph. "Is there something you want?"

She pulls the picture free and brings it closer to her failing eyes so she can examine the image. Running her crooked fingers over the youthful man with the thick black hair who was her husband, she whispers, "Are you okay?"

As the tears well in her eyes, she grabs the chair again and slowly pulls her aging body to a standing position. Turning to face the dog, she whispers, "Duke, my friend, I don't know for sure what's going on here, but I think our Albert has come back to us. It was exactly one year today since we lost him, but I think he's trying to tell us something."

When the dog does not respond, she turns to where the animal had been standing near the staircase. "Duke?"

She sees the dog is now lying on the floor. "Duke?" she cries, moving toward the animal. "Are you okay?"

Reaching the dog, she sees that he is not moving … and he's not breathing.

"Oh my," she sighs. "It was Duke, wasn't it," she whispers, glancing down at the picture she's holding in her hands. "You came to take Duke, didn't you?"

Grabbing the banister and lowering herself to her knees, Martha rubs her fragile hands through the dog's wiry fur and marvels at how still the animal has become.

"Go in peace, my friend," she whispers as the tears drip from her tired eyes. "You are together now. It's what you both wanted."

Meet Edna at the Boscawen Inn

Renowned for being the birthplace of the famous *Bluenose* and *Bluenose II*, the Town of Lunenburg has a long, proud seafaring history, replete with wooden ships, iron men and lots of ghost stories.

According to the provincial government's website, the first mention of a settlement in what would later become the Town of Lunenburg was in the early 1600s. At that time, it was an Acadian/Mi'kmaw village named Mirligueche. In the wake of recurring hostilities between the French and English, Nova Scotia's governor, Edward Cornwallis, ordered the village of wooden houses destroyed. In its place, a British fortress was erected to guard the harbour.

Foreign Protestants were encouraged to settle the area in a town that would be named Lunenburg, in honour of King George II, Duke of Brunschweig-Lunenburg.

Lunenburg would quickly become known as a major shipbuilding centre with local mills supplying the wood needed to build some of the most impressive sailing ships ever designed. Among these vessels was the famous *Bluenose*, a fishing and racing schooner built in 1921 that would remain undefeated in international racing for 17 years.

The *Bluenose* lives on today on the back of the Canadian dime, while her replica, the *Bluenose II*, has gone on to act as Nova Scotia's sailing ambassador around the world and continues to call Lunenburg home.

Today, Lunenburg is very much a town where the past meets the present. An impressive 70 percent of the original buildings from the 18th and 19th centuries continue to stand. As a result, the town has been recognized as a UNESCO World Heritage Site — a fitting tribute to the lasting history nestled alongside this tranquil harbour.

With so much history in the town, one would expect to find a few tales of the macabre and the odd ghost story hiding within the hallowed halls and walls of the centuries-old buildings that make up the world-renowned settlement.

And that's exactly what you will find at the Boscawen Inn, where a ghost by the name of Edna is said to roam the premises. An architectural landmark named for Admiral Edward Boscawen, the Queen Ann-style mansion on the hillside, overlooks Lunenburg Harbour and the Old Town below.

With the sea beyond and the leafy shade of Parade Square Park in its backyard, the Boscawen Inn is a special place, filled with history and, it would seem, spirits from the other side.

This 16-room Victorian mansion was built in 1888 by Senator H.A.N. Kaulbach, one of the most influential figures in Lunenburg's history, as a wedding present for his daughter, Edna, and son-in-law, James R. Rudolf. The mansion was designed by famed architect Henry Bush of Halifax and is Lunenburg's best example of the Queen Anne style of architecture.

This 16-room Victorian mansion was built in 1888 by Senator H.A.N. Kaulbach, one of the most influential figures in Lunenburg's history, as a wedding present for his daughter, Edna, and son-in-law, James R. Rudolf.

Edna and James lived in the impressive home where they raised three children. It was said that they were never truly happy there because James had a gambling problem and in time, they found themselves in debt to the point that they sold the home and moved south to take up residency near Boston. The couple never fully gave up their Nova Scotian connection, however, as they maintained a small summer cottage near Chester, just down the coast from Lunenburg.

But the Boscawen changed hands, having been purchased in 1945 by a Lunenburg businessman, Dana Sweeny, who carried out an extensive renovation and addition to the inn bringing it to its current configuration. The premises have operated as an inn and guest house ever since.

Enter the current owners, Judy and Jon Rawdon.

The Rawdons bought Boscawen in 2012, after years of dreaming of owning an inn. They were both accountants but, as Judy tells it, from their very first date they were making plans to find a property somewhere in the world that they could operate as an inn.

Judy who, with her husband Jon Rawdon, currently owns and operates Boscawen Inn. They are familiar with the ghost stories that surround their property.

Judy, from London, Ontario, met Jon when she moved to South Africa for a job and they eventually married. They spent their honeymoon touring around many countries including New Zealand and England, looking for the perfect place they could call home and to operate their business.

Then, Judy says, as if it was meant to be, early in 2012 while Jon was searching the Internet looking for potential places to purchase, he discovered a listing for the Boscawen Inn.

"He showed it to me and said, 'What about this place?' I was instantly hooked."

By May of 2012, the couple flew to Nova Scotia to look at two locations that they felt would suit their needs — one in Annapolis Royal and the second was the Boscawen.

"We fell in love with it right away," Judy says. "We instantly felt at home here and knew right away that we had found our dream property."

The couple returned to South Africa and began the process of securing the inn. On July 1, 2012, the Rawdons became proud owners of the historic Lunenburg property and they relocated to the seaside town by the fall of that year.

"And we've never looked back," she says. "We love it here and we're very, very happy here."

Even though the couple undertook extensive refurbishments of the structure, they were careful to maintain the property's historic integrity that is part of its character and charm.

"This place has a lot of history," Judy continues. "And we took great care to maintain that history. It was that history that attracted us to the property in the first place. Why would we change that?"

Along with the Boscawen's colourful history comes a local legend that the inn is possessed by the spirit of its original owner — Edna Kaulbach-Rudolf. There have been many reports over the years of guests, staff and visitors seeing Edna roaming the hallways of the stately mansion. Judy admits they had heard the stories before they purchased the place, but that did not deter them.

"Of course we were warned about the ghost when we were checking out the inn. This place has a lot of history and the ghosts are part of that history," she concedes. "But we're practical people and we thought, 'What's one little ghost in a beautiful place like this?' Besides, we've dealt with ghosts before when we were in South Africa so we are up for this one."

Since purchasing the Boscawen in 2012, Judy says they have heard many stories about Edna haunting the inn and while some of the stories seem pretty far-fetched, she agrees that some are too good to easily dismiss.

Shortly after they took ownership of the inn and moved in, Judy says they were told that one room — 202 — seems to be especially active when it comes to spiritual activity.

"One of our staff members has an especially inter-esting time in that room, hearing and seeing things connected to a rocking chair that's in there," Judy ex-plains. "It doesn't seem like that chair will stop rocking. It's like it's in constant motion."

And Room 303 in particular has a lot of traffic. The room has two single guest beds and it's known to be a hot spot for spiritual activity.

"This one night we had two women staying in the room and at some time through the night one of the women woke up and saw a woman in a white nightgown standing by the window and looking out over the harbour. She thought it was her friend with whom she was sharing the room."

The next morning, however, when the woman asked her friend if she had difficulty sleeping the previous night, her friend insisted she had slept soundly and had never gotten out of bed.

For the first woman, though, this left a mystery — if her friend was sound asleep in the other bed, then who was the woman in a white nightgown standing by the window?

Who indeed?

This mansion was designed by famed architect Henry Bush of Halifax and is Lunenburg's best example of the Queen Anne style of architecture. It's also said that one of the previous owners, Edna Kaulbach-Rudolf, still roams the halls.

"Strange things like this happen all the time in Room 303," Judy continues. "Our housekeeping staff will report that they've gone into the room after it's been cleaned only to find all the covers on the beds pulled back. This happens after the staff are certain they made up the beds."

And don't even get her started on the doors that seem to open and close all the time on their own.

"There is simply no explanation for that," she says. "But there are lots of things that happen in there that can't easily be explained, like the feeling that you're never really alone in there or that you can sometimes hear footsteps in the room when there is no one else in there with you."

Through it all, Judy says, she, her family, staff and guests never feel threatened or intimidated by whatever shares the inn with them.

"I feel it here. Other people feel it here, but no one feels that whoever or whatever is here means to cause any harm," Judy says.

Judy and others who have witnessed the paranormal activity at Boscawen Inn are convinced that the spirit that roams the halls and rooms of the mansion is that of a female and while they cannot know for certain if it's Edna, they believe it must be her as she was known to love the place.

"If it's Edna," Judy says, "then she's welcome to make herself at home and she's welcome to stay as long as she wants."

No One Walks Alone

Emily knew all the rules. The 47-year-old Windsor resident, who grew up in the Shelburne area on the province's South Shore, says she remembers the events of that August night in 1984 as if it was only yesterday.

From an early age, she says, her parents taught her not to talk to strangers and she practised what they told her. She considers herself to have been street smart and even today she says she is constantly aware of her surroundings.

"Old habits die hard," Emily says. "It's not that my parents were trying to frighten me and my sisters but they wanted to make sure we were prepared for anything so when they talked, I listened."

For as far back as she can remember, she was told about the dangers of talking to strangers and going with people she didn't know. She's sure she would never have done that as a child, not even in the small town where she was familiar with a lot of people, or at least saw people everyday who she could easily recognize. However, thanks to her parents, she was always mindful of possible dangers. As such, she was cautious, especially when she was out on her own.

Her parents insisted that she and her sisters should always be with each other or with a friend, especially in the evening hours, but Emily points out that was not always possible.

"It was really hard when I got older and wanted to be with my friends," she explains. "My sisters weren't always with me."

But when she found herself in a situation where she was alone, she remembered what her parents taught her. She avoided dark streets and high bushes, stayed where there was lots of light, always walked in neighbourhoods where there were lots of homes and she stuck to familiar areas. And she would never, under any circumstances, get into a vehicle unless it was with someone she knew very well and then, only if her parents had given her explicit permission to be in the company of this person.

While she thinks her parents did an excellent job teaching her and her sisters of the possible dangers that might lurk around every corner, she understands the delicate balancing act they faced. She knows they didn't want to make her so afraid that she would not go outside or so intimidated that she would avoid people altogether. She understands there are dangers in the world and there are people who will take advantage of children, especially when they are alone and at their most vulnerable state, but she believes it's also important that children learn how to associate with people because they cannot live in a bubble.

Emily knows her parents, both of whom have now passed away, meant well. But as she matured, she often felt like telling them they couldn't wrap her and her sisters in a cocoon.

"I'm sure that they understood that things happen no matter what precautions you take," Emily says. "No matter what you do, there are people out there who always try to do the opposite and I know Mom and Dad were always trying to protect us from those kind of people."

So she took heed of those lessons and followed her parents' instructions to the letter, even whenever she was at a friend's house and it became time for her to go home after supper. She always timed her departure so that she could be home before it got dark.

Emily and her best friend, Amanda, spent most of their time between each other's homes, which were separated by a 15-minute walk, and they knew the route they always travelled very well. Emily had it timed perfectly so that whenever she was at her friend's home, she could leave and arrive at her own house in about 12 minutes if she went quickly and didn't talk to anyone. Before leaving Amanda's home she made it a habit to phone ahead and let her parents know she was on her way.

Maybe she was being a little paranoid, she concedes, but it only took a minute to call ahead and it made her feel comfortable that her parents knew she was on her way so they could watch for her. Sometimes one of her parents would even offer to come and meet her, but as she got older, she decided that was no longer necessary. However, she still phoned them and told them that she was on her way. Maybe it was just a courtesy, but in a way it also made her feel better knowing that if she wasn't home within a reasonable time, her mom or dad would come looking for her.

However, on this particular August night in 1984, when she phoned home she was surprised when no one answered. Then she remembered her parents telling her they were likely going to drop by the hospital to visit a sick relative and that they might not be at the house when she was ready to come home. They had also told her they would make sure there was a key in the secret hiding place out in the back shed.

She also remembered her mom had told her that they would not be late, that she should get the key from the shed, come inside, lock the door behind her and not open it for anyone.

Listening as the phone rang, Emily recalls she was somewhat nervous thinking about going home alone to an empty house, especially because it was getting dark, but she also felt she was growing up and could handle the responsibility.

There was no question that she could have remained at Amanda's house until she was certain her mom and dad had returned, but she figured she was now old enough to handle this on her own so she headed for home. Amanda's mom had also kindly offered to walk with her, but she told her she was fine and off she went.

Thinking back, she remembers she walked quickly down the sidewalk, which was otherwise empty, the cool breeze tossing her long brown hair about her head. She admits she was scared thinking about the idea of heading home alone. She had taken this route hundreds, if not thousands of times, over the years and she thinks she could have probably followed the sidewalk with her eyes closed.

But, she points out, it's the little things about being alone that frightened her and by the time she reached the halfway point, she had managed to work herself into such a tizzy that she began to regret her decision to leave Amanda's place. However, she knew it was too late to turn back since she was just about home.

Maybe it was the idea of being on the street by herself, or perhaps it was the thought of going home to an empty house, or maybe it was the memories of all the stories she had heard over the years about strangers and little kids, but the farther Emily got from her friend's house, the more nervous she became. If only she had someone to walk with her, she thought.

As the evening's light continued to fade into night, Emily remembers that she began to shiver, as she suddenly felt very alone and vulnerable. She hated that feeling.

"Come on, Emily," she told herself, moving quickly down the street toward her home. "You can do this. You're old enough to handle this. You're 11, almost a teenager. It's time to grow up."

She was so wrapped up in her thoughts that by the time she sensed the presence beside her, it was too late to avoid contact.

Glancing over her right shoulder, she was startled to see an older man suddenly walking directly behind her, but she was relieved that while maintaining his pace, he was also keeping his distance. She had no idea where he had come from or who the man was. She doesn't remember recognizing him as being from the neighbourhood, but as she turned around and got a good, clear look at his wrinkled face, he returned the biggest, warmest smile she had ever seen.

Although this man was a total stranger, in no way did she feel threatened or afraid of him. If anything, she suddenly felt very warm toward the old man, even though she had no idea who he was.

"Where are you heading?" the man asked her. His voice was friendly, almost soothing. Surprisingly, his words sounded full of life even though he looked very old.

"Home," she told him, immediately thinking she should not be talking to him. She feared her parents would be very disappointed if they knew she was doing that, but it was as if she felt compelled to speak.

"By yourself?" he asked. His voice was soft.

"My house is just up the street a little ways and my mom and dad are waiting there for me," she told him, even though she knew her parents were not at home.

"Very good," the old man replied. "You are a brave young girl to be out here by yourself just before dark."

"I'm not afraid," she answered.

As they talked, Emily and the strange man continued along their route, with him keeping his distance, several steps behind her but keeping in perfect time with her, step for step.

"It is a very nice evening," she remembers the old man saying

"Yes. It is," she agreed, while keeping her eyes glued on the man. She was prepared to make a run for safety if he made one wrong move toward her. She was sure she could put some distance between them if she had to.

"I like these late summer evenings," he continued to say. "They are not too hot and it's starting to cool off."

"I like them too, but it means summer's almost over and we will soon be heading back to school." Emily still vividly remembers the conversation.

"Yes, I suppose it does," he agreed.

"But I like school," she remembers telling him.

"That is good," he replied.

In short order, Emily realized that she had reached her destination and announced, "I'm here. This is my house."

She recalls him saying, "Very well." And then, just as suddenly as he appeared, the old man was gone.

At that point she could see that her mother had been standing on the front doorstep awaiting her arrival.

"We just this minute pulled into the yard, Emily," her mom said as she greeted her daughter by the front door. "You made out okay coming from Amanda's house?"

"Yes," Emily said to her mother. "I was a little frightened at first but about halfway here I met this nice old man who walked the rest of the way with me until I got here to the walkway. I know he was a stranger but I could tell right away that he was okay. You must have seen him."

"Seen who?" Emily remembers that her mother appeared puzzled by what she had told her.

"You must have seen the nice old man that was walking behind me," Emily explained. "We were talking about the weather and about school. I know he was a stranger and I should not talk to strangers, but he seemed very friendly. He was just there a minute ago."

Appearing lost for words, her mother finally said, "Emily, honey, I've been standing here for the last few minutes and I watched you come up the sidewalk. Do you honestly believe that if I had seen you talking to a strange man that I wouldn't have said something to you?"

"No," Emily answered, throwing a puzzled glance at her mother. "I guess not."

"There was no man behind you," her mother told her. "I would have seen him. … You were all alone."

"No, Mom," she insisted. "There was a man with me."

"I don't know what to tell you, Emily, but I did not see any man with you," her mother replied, opening the front door. "You must have been really nervous and just imagined him."

"Okay, maybe you didn't see him," Emily told her mother. "But I'm telling you, he was there."

"Fine, Emily," her mother finally said. "Let's go inside. It's getting late and it's time to get ready for bed."

At that point, Emily remembers that both she and her mother dropped the subject, but even to this day, all these years later, she cannot get the image of that nice, old man out of her mind. She's sure he was there and she felt really comfortable … and safe with him.

Maybe, she thinks, he was her guardian angel, but whatever the case, she knows she was not walking alone that night and she never forgot how safe he made her feel.

A few years later, as she and her mother were going through some old family photographs, Emily was caught off guard when she turned over a picture and there he was. Staring up at her from the torn and tattered photo was the same old man who had walked with her that night.

"I'm positive it was the same man," she says, "and I quickly asked Mom who he was but she didn't know for sure, as these particular photos were in a box that her own mother had passed onto her before she died.

"But it must have been a relative or someone close to the family," Emily concludes. "The question is, why did he walk with me that night and why have I never seen him again?"

Both good questions, indeed.

A Mother's Intuition

Call it a gut feeling. Call it a sixth sense. Or call it intuition, but have you ever known something with certainty, even though you can't explain how you know it?

It is possible that all of us have the gift of intuition, but only a few are able to tap into it. Mothers, though, are highly intuitive, especially when it comes to the wellbeing of their children.

There have been many documented cases of mothers intuitively knowing when their children were in trouble, even when great distances have separated them. Many a time a mother has felt a strong urge to reach out to her child and followed that instinct only to find her child was in distress.

Helen and her husband Arthur had three children, all boys. Arthur was a fisherman who had toiled on the North Atlantic his entire life and while he earned a good, honest living from the sea, he would be the first to agree that it was also a hard life. The days were long and the conditions were dangerous, with Arthur having survived many close calls during his lifetime.

Working on the sea was all Arthur knew and like his own father and all the men from his family who came before him, he was content with the life he had created for his family. Be that as it may, however, it wasn't a life that he wanted for any of his boys. He hoped his children would grow up and find jobs that would provide a good lifestyle for their own families but as fate would have it, all three of Arthur's sons followed him to sea and all three were happy and content to do so.

Helen worried about her sons, naturally. She had spent her entire married life worrying and fretting over the safety of her husband and as each of her sons grew up and took to the open sea, she took on the burden of worry for each of them as well.

It was a heavy load to carry on her shoulders. She knew first-hand the perils of the life of a fisherman as she had lost many members of her own family to tragedies on the ocean, including her older brother.

She waited with bated breath each and every time Arthur or any of her sons went to sea. It was not easy to remain ashore not knowing what her loved ones were facing so many miles out on the open seas. She coped and prayed, accepting that such was the life of a fisherman's wife and mother.

Helen had a deep bond with all three of her sons, but that bond ran deepest with her youngest son, Jimmy. Perhaps it was that bond or her intuition that led her to know something was wrong in 1996, long before she knew all the facts.

As her two oldest sons grew up, married and moved out of the house to start their own families, Jimmy remained behind and lived with his parents. That arrangement was just fine with Helen. She knew the day would come when her son would meet someone and move out, but she was prepared to pepper her youngest child with as much love and affection as she could while he was still at home.

She liked having her son around the house, but she loathed those times when he went to sea for she feared he might not return. Sometimes, as the job demanded, Jimmy would be gone for four or five days at a time and those long trips were especially hard on his mother.

When he wasn't fishing, Jimmy liked to party and, as many young men do, he would go out with his friends, sometimes not returning home until late into the night. This, of course, caused Mom to worry and she spent many a sleepless night wondering what her youngest son was up to and if he was okay.

Helen didn't sleep much when Jimmy was out with his friends and because he was still living under her roof, she had one rule that she insisted he follow. She didn't ask any questions because her son was an adult, but no matter what time he came in at night, she insisted that he come to tell her that he was home and that everything was okay.

Knowing how much this meant to his mother, Jimmy followed the rule and whenever he came home, no matter the time, he would go directly to his parents' bedroom, stand in the doorway and announce that he was okay. With that reassurance from her son, Helen was able to fall asleep.

Sometimes the hour was very late and while he hated to bother them, he also knew his mother would not be sleeping. While the routine was borne from the elderly woman's worries about her son's well-being, in time, it kind of became a running joke between the two, but no matter how old Jimmy became he continued the practice for many years.

Shortly after Jimmy's 26th birthday, he was preparing for a fishing trip that his captain estimated would last four or five days. Including the captain, there were four crewmembers on board and Jimmy brought home a good payday for his long hours of work.

He was looking forward to this trip because he was saving money for a down payment on a house that he had been eyeing and he estimated that these earnings would give him enough to finally make the purchase. But while he was looking forward to the trip, his mother was dreading it.

In the days leading up to her son's departure, she couldn't shake the feeling that something was terribly wrong. She couldn't quite explain it, but she felt there was a dark cloud hanging over her family and she feared something terrible was about to happen. Because her husband had since retired and neither of her older sons was scheduled to go out in the near future, she couldn't shake the feeling that whatever was about to happen must involve Jimmy.

Fearing the worst, she tried for days to convince Jimmy to skip this trip, telling him that he didn't need the money and offering to pay whatever difference he needed for his down payment on the house. But Jimmy wasn't having any of that and as he packed his gear, he dismissed his mother's fears as nothing more than the ramblings of a superstitious old woman.

On the morning of his departure, he kissed his mother goodbye as he always did, and told her he would see her in four or maybe five days. As he left through the kitchen, he paused at the back door and turned back to tell her not to worry. He insisted he would be okay.

But Helen was not so sure about that and as she watched her youngest son walk down the back steps and disappear down the back walkway on his way to the wharf, she felt a deep gnawing in the pit of her stomach.

Something was wrong, she believed, fearing she would never see her son again.

As the next two days crept by, the dark cloud followed Helen wherever she went. She could not shake the oppressive feeling that tragedy was near. She prayed that her son and his fellow crewmembers were okay and that they would make it safely back to port.

On the night of the second day of Jimmy's trip, Helen was having an especially difficult time sleeping. Tossing and turning, she remembers glancing at the digital clock on the night table next to her bed. In glowing red numbers, the clock said it was 12:15 a.m.

Just then, she felt a strong urge to turn around and when she did, she was surprised to see Jimmy standing in the doorway. He said to her, "Don't worry, Mom. Everything is okay. You can go to sleep now."

While Helen was surprised to see Jimmy standing there, because he wasn't due back in port for at least another two days, perhaps even three, as a fisherman's wife she also knew that many things can happen out at sea that may force the boat to return earlier than scheduled.

Perhaps there was engine trouble. Perhaps the catch was good and they filled their hold early. Perhaps someone was sick or injured and needed medical attention. Perhaps there was a storm at sea that they didn't know about back on land. Whatever was going on, Helen took comfort in knowing that Jimmy was home and, knowing that she could get the details from him in the morning, she rolled over and went to sleep.

The next morning, as Helen and Arthur were in the kitchen having breakfast, the telephone rang. She quickly picked up the receiver after the first ring because she didn't want the noise to wake her son.

As Helen spoke to whoever was on the phone, Arthur knew something was wrong as he watched his wife turn every shade of white he could imagine. Quickly placing her hand over the phone, she told him to go up stairs and check on Jimmy.

Without questioning his wife's instructions, Arthur immediately went up the stairs. Upon his return a few minutes later, he informed his wife that Jimmy was not in his bed and furthermore, it didn't look like anyone had slept in the bed last night.

"No," Helen cried, dropping the phone. She insisted that Jimmy had come last night and that he had spoken to her.

Picking up the phone, Arthur listened while one of the captains from the wharf told him that Jimmy's boat was missing and that they had no contact with them since — are you ready for it — 12:15 a.m.

According to the man from the wharf, that was the last time that any known transmission was sent from Jimmy's boat and it was feared that the boat and all four crewmembers had been lost.

But how could that be? That's a question that haunted Helen in the years following the tragedy.

"I knew something was wrong," she said. "I knew Jimmy was in trouble long before that boat went down."

Had Helen seen Jimmy's forerunner, a celestial image of a person in distress or imminent danger? Did the young man reach out to his mother during the last few minutes of his life to let her know he was okay?

Helen went to her grave thinking yes, indeed, that is exactly what happened.

Bodies Buried under Liverpool Streets

There is a long-held legend in the privateering seaport of Liverpool, located on Nova Scotia's South Shore, that the bodies of two dearly departed men are buried beneath two of the town's streets.

And, in fact, there is some historical documentation to confirm these legends, that while strange, are actually more fact than fiction.

It is recorded in the famous Simeon Perkins diary that William Brocklesby died on December 13, 1799. Brocklesby, a reformed alcoholic, worked as a mason and had quit drinking two and a half years prior to his suicide. But he got "in with privateers people at Mrs [sic] Boyles," Perkins writes and he was on a drinking binge of about one week before his death.

He died by hanging himself in John Robert's barn, located near Weir Lane behind the building at what is now 325-327 Main Street.

In those times, people who died by their own hands were not permitted to be buried in hallowed ground. Following Brocklesby's death, a coroner's inquest was held and Brocklesby was subsequently "buryed [sic] in the lane by the burying ground."

Today, this lane is known as Old Bridge Street.

According to local legend, a man by the name of William Brocklesby is buried under this Liverpool street. Now known as Old Bridge Street, the road forms the border of the town's historic old burying ground.

While explicit details of the second body are not as well known or documented as the first, according to legend a young soldier — perhaps a member of the famed King's Orange Rangers who defended the privateering port at this juncture in history — reportedly hanged himself in Perkins' apple orchard located near the top of Hop Toad Hill after receiving a Dear John letter from the woman he loved.

Today, this area is the location of Queens General Hospital and the Queens RCMP detachment.

Because the young soldier took his own life, it is said that his body was buried under the road located at the foot of the hill. Several hundred years ago, the road would have been nothing more than a wagon path. Based on today's coordinates, however, that location would be somewhere in the area of the four-way intersection of School and Waterloo Streets.

So what's the story here?

The practice of burying bodies under the streets and roads of early settlements originated in Europe and dates back many centuries. As it was a sin to take one's own life, the deceased could not be buried in hallowed ground and furthermore, because of the nature of the death, it was believed the spirit of the deceased would be restless and would want to roam. It was believed that the traffic from the street (path or trail) would force the spirit to remain planted in the ground and as such, the practice came with the settlers of the new world.

In some instances, the practice of burying the deceased in the streets also included burying the body face down and in more extreme cases, driving a wooden stake through the body to keep the spirit pinned in place. Strange, but true.

Photo by Vernon Oickle

As the story goes, the body of a man who committed suicide hundreds of years earlier, is said to be buried somewhere near this intersection and under the pavement.

The Ghosts of Chestnut Holler

In ghost lore, a haunted house or ghosthouse is a house or other building often perceived as being inhabited by disembodied spirits of the deceased who may have been former residents or were familiar with the property.

Parapsychologists attribute hauntings to the spirits of the dead and the effect of violent or tragic events in the building's past such as murder, accidental death or suicide.

One recent poll suggests that 28 percent of Canadians believe in haunted houses and you can count Jamie Symonds of Barrington as one of those believers. He is certain that he shares his ancestral home with at least one spirit, perhaps even several.

In 1891, a family with the surname Pyke built the house, located on Villagedale Road in Barrington. The house ended up in Symonds' family's ownership in 1920 when his great grandparents paid $300 for the property, purchasing it in a tax sale. The home has remained in the family ever since.

Jamie recalls visiting the house throughout his childhood and even then, although he doesn't ever recall witnessing any paranormal activity at that time, he does remember thinking there was something really "unusual" about the place.

"I couldn't exactly put my finger on it," he explains, "but you know what it's like when you just have this feeling that there's something strange about a place even though you can't see it or touch it. That's what it was like. You could sense it, you could feel it all around you, or at least I could."

Photo by Vernon Oickle

This beautiful home located on Villagedale Road in Barrington and known as Chestnut Holler Guesthouse was built in 1891.

As an adult, Jamie moved to the US to work as a software engineer, but eventually he purchased the family home in Barrington and used it as a summer retreat. In 2016, as modern technology allowed him to work remotely, Jamie moved back to Barrington where he and his partner, Cameron, settled permanently in the family home.

That's when things began to get really strange, Jamie points out, explaining that the house does have some dark history associated with it.

Jamie Symonds welcomes guests to the historic Chestnut Holler Guesthouse.

"I am convinced there is a presence here," he insists, acknowledging that sometimes he hears and sees things that defy explanation.

But first, he explains it's important to understand that in the past, the house has been the location for some experiences that may explain why restless spirits would inhabit the premises.

For starters, he says, there was a suicide in the house, and there is a sad story of a six or seven-year-old girl with polio who was confined to the house because of her physical limitations. As well, a 40-year-old uncle of Jamie's dropped dead one day in the yard without warning. He died of a sudden heart attack, or at least that's the common assumption.

This uncle, Jamie explains, had schizophrenia and was known to be in a real bad way. He did not want to be around other people and so he remained holed up in the house where his seclusion only added to his dementia.

Jamie says he has heard many stories about his uncle but one he specifically remembers is that the man didn't allow clocks in the house. "He thought the clocks on the walls were eyes and they would follow him around the house."

That is kind of creepy, he concedes.

Even to this day, Jamie admits, when he's in the house he sometimes glances at the clocks just to see if anyone is looking back. He chuckles at the notion, but quickly adds, "I know it may sound weird to some people but there are times when you can sense something in this house."

Truthfully, he continues, "I actually think there is more than one restless spirit in this place. I think there's two or maybe even three in the house because at different times, things just feel and sound different, which leads me to think there's more than one."

Since he has been here as an adult, Jamie says he has had many experiences that he cannot explain.

"For instance, it's very common for the cold water to start running in the bathtub located on the main floor even though no one is in the bathroom," he says, pointing out that's only one of the many strange occurrences that happen in the house.

And, he adds, it's all modern plumbing, so there is no way a tap should turn on by itself.

"Just like the water in the bathroom, it's not uncommon for the light in the pantry to come on by itself," Jamie says. "And tools and other things will just disappear never to be found again, even though you were just using them. That one really drives me nuts, especially when you know for certain that you just had the bloody thing in your hands."

While the happenings are not all confined to the main floor, Jamie says it does seem that the majority of incidents do happen on the ground level and mostly around the kitchen.

"It's weird when it happens," Jamie explains. "For instance, I was in the front part of the house where the living room is located when I heard someone come in the back door to the kitchen and yell, 'Hello. Is anyone home?' It was distinctly a male voice, I am 100 percent certain of that."

But when he went to check out who had come to visit, there was no one in the kitchen. And this sort of thing has happened on more than one occasion, Jamie says.

Photo by Vernon Oickle

A view of the home's front entrance from the second floor.

"Again, on another day, I was in the living room when I heard Cameron come in the back door to the kitchen and I heard him begin putting the groceries away," he pauses, shrugs and then continues. "I was certain it was Cameron that I heard but when I went into the kitchen to talk to him, there was no one else there. The place was empty and I thought I must be going crazy."

There have been many other strange occurrences in the house, Jamie points out, including the sound of footsteps on the second floor where the bedrooms are located. "Only when you go up to investigate, you can never find anyone. But the footsteps are loud enough to hear from downstairs so someone was walking around."

And other things convince him there is a presence in the house, he says, like seeing a cat that they don't have and, on one occasion, Jamie insists he saw a hand but no body, which was, he says, more than a little unnerving.

Another time, he continues, while he was in the living room, he heard someone shriek his name. "It wasn't a normal voice or even a yell," he explains. "It was like someone was shrieking in a very high pitched tone."

Despite all of these strange happenings that convince him there is a presence in the house, Jamie says through it all, he has never felt threatened or intimidated.

"Whatever is in the house, I really don't feel it means any harm to me or anyone else," he says. "True, it can be a little unsettling at times when things happen that you cannot easily explain, but I have never felt that there was any danger — never."

Courtesy Linda Rafuse

If you look closely at the bottom right pane of the kitchen window you may see a face looking back at you. Glances of figures in the house are fairly common.

A Bridge in Time

You could be standing on top of it and not even know it is there. But that doesn't mean the centuries old stone bridge in the centre of Chester isn't appreciated as a valuable and unique heritage structure. It also plays an integral role in one of the region's most popular ghost stories.

The village's historic stone bridge dates back to the 1880s. Although there are no precise records as to when it was constructed, it is known that the structure was built for horse carriages and then later expanded to carry two-way vehicular traffic. It measures roughly 18.28 meters in length and is reported to be one of only two Roman-style stone arch bridges still in use in the province.

A vestige of Nova Scotia's industrial past, records suggest, however, that the bridge was constructed around 1882 after the famed Saxby Gale of 1869 destroyed the original wooden bridge. Located on Victoria Street with Chester Back Harbour to its west and the Old Mill Race Stream to its east, the bridge carried horse carriages back and forth and at one time serviced Hawboldt's Foundry, a marine engine manufacturer founded by Chester inventor Forman Hawboldt in 1906.

Believed to be one of the oldest surviving stone arch bridges in Nova Scotia, the structure's age, rare architecture and historical ties all combine to make it special.

A testament to its sound design and structural integrity, the Old Stone Bridge has been in continual use for more than a century without any significant alterations.

Today, the bridge is designated as a provincial heritage site to protect the structure's historical integrity. But according to local folklore, the bridge also comes with a ghost. It is said that on some darkened, foggy nights, if one listens very closely, it is possible to hear someone splash out of the stream below, scramble up the embankment and then start the climb up the side of the bridge.

Some witnesses, on full-moon-lit nights, have even reported seeing a man climbing up the side of the bridge. But who is this man and where did he come from? Furthermore, how did he end up in the stream that flows under the historic stone bridge? And what is he chasing that it compels him to climb up the bridge?

Clues for answers to all of these questions may be found in a story shared by life-long Chester resident and local historian, Gail Smith. She admits that since she was a child growing up in the village, she heard all the stories and legends connected to the bridge. She believes the story begins in an old, long-gone house that, at one time, stood on property adjacent to the crossing where the bridge structure is located.

The house in question was built around 1710 by a French fisherman. One of the unique features of the house was that its basement was built using flagstone that came all the way from France and that was used as ballast in their ships. The house passed through many owners over the years until, eventually, her ancestors purchased it. Her own memories of the house begin when she was a youngster as she spent much of her time there.

"I remember that my father was born in the house," Gail explains, "so it was an important part of our family for many years. I remember visiting my grandmother there and sitting in the kitchen with her. And I remember strange things happening in that house all the time."

Those unexplained incidents included doors opening of their own accord, hearing footsteps in the kitchen when there was no one there and the stove lids rattling uncontrollably for no apparent reason.

"I remember my grandmother telling me when things like that happened that there was nothing to worry about and nothing seemed to phase her," Gail recalls. "When the doors would come open, she would close them and shrug it off, but I would not have spent a night alone in that house without my grandmother. It just would not have happened."

Despite the possibility of a ghostly inhabitant, Gail says she loved the house.

"It was a beautiful home with significant historical value," she adds. "I have a lot of great memories in that house."

After her grandmother died in 1959, Gail stopped visiting the house, but she always maintained her curiosity about the property. In fact, as an historian, she has done a great deal of research into the house.

It seems that according to historical records, the house had at one time been owned by a woman named Charlotte Mallock and between 1825 and 1850, she operated a dry goods store out of the house as well as a tavern.

In due time, the place developed quite a reputation. As the stagecoach would come into Chester, it would leave passengers there for a few libations. As the story goes, the booze flowed freely.

This is where the story gets really interesting.

According to local legend, a gentleman (more aptly described as a carpetbagger) by the name of Mr. Brown arrived at Mrs. Mallock's tavern one cold evening in February and joined a number of the local men folk for a few drinks and a friendly game of cards. As this was a tavern, it only stands to reason that liquor was plentiful throughout the game with gallons of spruce beer and rum flowing freely during the ensuing hours.

But as often happens when gamblers mix cards with liquor, and someone loses a large sum of money, accusations of cheating and skullduggery entered the picture.

And so it was on this particular night when the card players accused Mr. Brown — who appeared to be exceedingly lucky — of somehow cheating and pocketing his ill-gotten spoils.

As accusations flew, tempers flared and voices were raised. In due course, a pistol entered the picture and a shot rang out. When the smoke cleared and the kerfuffle became quiet, Mr. Brown lay on the hardwood floor, bleeding profusely. He was dead.

What to do with the body?

Since it was the middle of winter and the ground was frozen solid, burying the corpse was not an option. The only viable solution then was to drag the body down to the original wooden bridge and toss the remains of Mr. Brown into the Mill Pond, where the current would carry it downstream and into the ocean.

Or so the conspirators were betting. They knew it was a gamble.

Everyone present when Mr. Brown was shot to his death by a single bullet swore an oath never to reveal the truth of the matter and all went on his or her merry way, carrying the bloody secret with them.

So it came to pass that Mr. Brown faded into history and into local folklore.

When spring came, up from the icy water of Mill Pond rose the bloated corpse of Mr. Brown, which was subsequently discovered by passersby. Constables from the nearby town of Lunenburg were summoned to the location, where the decomposing corpse had been found.

Authorities immediately identified the missing man as a Mr. Brown from the Annapolis Valley. They promptly sent the remains home from whence he came as he had been reported missing since February.

Photo by Vernon Oickle

The historic stone bridge in Chester dates back to the 1880s and is the focal point of a long-running mysterious legend.

However, even though the body had been recovered, the conspiracy of silence that had been sworn the night of the murder held fast and the mystery around Mr. Brown's death was never solved. There were never any prosecutions or arrests.

In time, Mrs. Charlotte Mallock packed up all of her belongings and moved away never to be heard of again, her memory fading into the annals of local history.

Gail says while this all sounds like a good "story," she believes there may be at least some truth surrounding this version of events.

Over the years she heard stories of homeowners trying to scrub some sort of brown stains from the hardwood floor in the sitting room but they could never be removed. Could those have been stains from Mr. Brown's blood?

It is possible.

"When the house was about to be torn down, I got to see those stains firsthand," Gail says. "And honestly, I have no idea what they were but they most certainly could have been from blood."

The house is gone now but the legend of the ghost of the Chester stone bridge lives on, according to Gail.

"The story has been passed down for generations," she chuckles. "As kids, we would go to the bridge and call out the ghost of Mr. Brown. I guess we didn't know what to expect but it was a lot of childish fun."

But seriously, she adds, over the years she has heard numerous reports of people seeing someone climbing up the side of the old bridge and they insist it is, without a doubt, the outline of a man they are seeing.

Is it the spirit of Mr. Brown, the salesman who was shot and killed in the old house while playing cards that cold February night so many years ago?

Maybe, but who can really say for sure?

The Mysterious Guest

Spirits move in mysterious ways, oftentimes defying simple explanation and sometimes showing up in places you wouldn't expect them to be. It is a common belief, however, that spirits can be connected to a person, place or thing. And Linda Attaway, who lives in Chester on Nova Scotia's beautiful South Shore, believes she has proof of that theory.

On October 31, 2015, Linda and her husband Ken moved into their 150 to 175-year-old home located in Middle LaHave, a small picturesque village on the outskirts of Bridgewater, the region's largest town. And almost immediately, they agree, they felt there was something "a little off" about the property, something they just could not explain.

"It was Halloween and maybe that should have been a clue," Linda begins. "We were busy moving things around and getting things settled into the house, when Ken says to me, 'Why are you playing Christmas music? It's the wrong holiday.' But I wasn't playing Christmas music and I had no idea where it was coming from. I didn't hear it at first, but when I stopped and listened, I could hear it as well."

Even though the pair searched the house from top to bottom, trying to determine where the music was coming from, they had no luck in locating the source although they were inexplicably drawn to a Christmas decoration hanging in an upstairs closet. But they can't say for sure whether that's where the music originated.

Furthermore, the couple adds, the incident on October 31 was just the first of many Christmas-themed events they encountered over the next few months, leading up to the holiday season.

During that period, they not only continued to hear the music playing at various intervals, but on more than one occasion, they distinctly heard a man's voice saying, "Merry Christmas, Ho, Ho, Ho."

The deep voice was very clear, they agree, but the source remained a mystery.

In addition to the music and voices, Ken says that on more than one occasion they experienced objects going missing and never being found again. Several times, he felt someone poke him in the back when, in fact, there was no one else in the room with him.

"It was like someone was trying to get my attention," he says. "Which they certainly did."

While Linda and Ken admit that experiencing such things without being able to locate their source was a bit disconcerting, they never felt intimidated or threatened in any way while in the house.

"But it was unusual," Linda nods. "It certainly was strange, I'll give you that much."

As for Ken, he says that in addition to the unusual phenomena they were experiencing in the house, they felt that there was something unusual about the house and, whatever it was, it was trying to get their attention.

"We certainly had a feeling that there was something else in the house, that's for sure," he says. "We never saw anything, but we just *felt* it … we could sense it."

As the couple continued to settle into their new home, Linda sought to immerse herself in her painting, a hobby she had enjoyed for many years. While they were moving into the house, she had been working on a painting of daisies, which she ultimately decided she didn't like.

"I had painted this horrible painting of daisies," Linda says. "Not wishing to keep it but being practical as a poor starving artist, I decided to cover it up with a mixture of oil paints so I could use the board again."

With surgical gloves on her hands and an array of oil paints at her disposal, she smeared the daisies over with random paints. The result of mixed paint left a canvas in hues of oranges, browns and some red.

"As I often will do in such cases, I rotated the canvas to see if perhaps an image might want to present itself," she continues. "Not surprisingly … an image did want to rise up through the many layers of paint to make itself known."

She began scratching the burdened-down canvas with a pallet knife.

"I could see an image of a man's face," Linda says. "I went with that until it began to resemble more and more the face of a man both old and, yet, also young."

Working over a few days, redoing the eyes — open, shut, and then open again — "Mysterious Guest" was finished in December. The eyes are the most eerie part of the piece, she says.

In this case, Linda says, the new image just occurred, but the man in the painting didn't look like anyone she or Ken knew.

"It began to bother me as to the man's identity, for I felt that he was someone wishing to make his presence known," she says. "He emerged up out of a mess with a smile and moving eyes, but who was he?"

Linda Attaway with the painting she calls *Mysterious Guest*.

Since Linda and Ken were living in a very old house, which had sat empty for more than 45 years before they moved in, surely he was a past resident, she assumed. Yet, everyone she asked about the man in the painting could not recognize him, nor did he resemble the original owner's photo. This was, indeed, a mystery!

Linda explains the story took a most unusual and profound turn in February of the following year when she noticed that a fellow artist named Mara from Florida, whom she has never met in person, lost her husband, Bob. Without warning, he just dropped dead at a concert he was performing in.

Following her husband's death, Mara posted several photos of Bob to Facebook. Seeing those photos, Linda was struck by the uncanny resemblance of the deceased man's face and that of the man in her "Mysterious Guest" painting.

"It took me three months and much encouragement to approach Mara with my observation as I didn't know how she would react. But Mara's response was so positive, every word dripping in tears. She confirmed that the man in "Mysterious Guest" was Bob, that as a young man when they first met, he had worn his hair like Bill Clinton. His eyebrows and moustache were so wiry that she was perpetually trimming them."

The resemblance is undeniable.

Photo by Vernon Oickle

This painting of a man Linda had never met, emerged on her canvas.

"It looks like Bob wanted to speak to Mara after his death," Linda says. "What he wanted to say, I don't know, and … why he chose me to be the catalyst for communication is beyond me — but he did."

In time, Mara eventually confessed to Linda that she had always wanted to do a portrait of Bob but thought she needed to take a course from certain other artists first before tackling the project.

Photo by Mara Trumbo

This is what Bob Trumbo looked like.

"If she had done it, I am sure her version would have had more realism."

But, Linda wonders, is it possible that Bob knew about Mara's desire to paint him and this was a gift meant for her?

"Mara wanted to exchange paintings so she could have mine. However, the story behind 'Mysterious Guest' has such a profound appreciation with me that giving him away would be giving away the evidence of my story."

And there's no denying it's an unusual story.

"We had no idea who the man in the painting was," she says. "But the image of the stranger just seemed to weep up through the paint until you could clearly see him. He has very distinct qualities, especially his eyes, and his moustache and hair are very distinct. We just didn't know who he was."

As a painter, Linda says she knows it's not unusual to be inspired by things that don't seem normal, but usually she paints things and subjects with which she is familiar.

In this case, however, that was not so. Linda couldn't help feeling there was something unusual about the man in the painting, especially considering that most of the strange phenomena Linda and Ken had been experiencing had seemed to centre around a man.

Photo by Mara Trumbo

This is Mara and Bob Trumbo. Prior to her mysterious painting, Linda Attaway had no previous contact with the Florida-based couple.

Were the strange incidents somehow connected to the man in the painting? That's a good question, both Linda and Ken agree. However, it's one they cannot definitively answer.

In truth, the man in the painting could be nothing more than a figment of Linda's imagination and the undeniable resemblance of the man in the painting to the man in the photos could be nothing more than a coincidence. But if you believe in the unexplainable, then there is one plausible explanation.

"There is an uncanny resemblance of the two men. It's as if they are the same person," Linda says. "Somehow, I painted a man from Florida I had never met three months before he died."

Was it a coincidence or something more? And was there a connection to the house in Middle LaHave? If so, what was that connection? The man from Florida had never been there.

Sometimes, there are no simple explanations for the way in which the universe moves and considering their experiences in the house, perhaps there is a connection … on another dimension. Maybe, but whatever the case, Linda and Ken sold the house and moved to Chester in August 2017.

"We didn't know the history of that house, but we could sense that there was something unusual about it," Linda says, adding that even though they never felt like they were in any danger, they decided the house just wasn't a good fit for them.

The Haunted Bog

There is a place near the Town of Liverpool on Nova Scotia's South Shore that locals call The Haunted Bog. The Mi'kmaq had their own name for the mystical place. Years ago, they called it "Indian Devil Country."

Almost 25 kilometres north of Liverpool and just slightly west of the Mersey River can be found a trio of lakes — Eagle, Kempton and Long (also known as Toney) lakes. Together, these lakes form a triangle and within that triangle can be found a variety of geographic features including dense forests of pine, nearly impassable rocky terrain, ridges and gorges, streams teeming with trout and countless bogs, meadows and watershed areas. The landscape is as varied as one could imagine.

Centuries ago, the region had been exploited and ravaged by land barons through wasteful practices that were common in their time. They dammed the rivers with wooden structures and felled the towering trees, turning the forest floor into a virtual wasteland. The lumbering process practically devastated the once rich forests, sending wildlife scampering in search of new homes and leaving the fish floundering in dammed-up waterways, cut off from their ancestral swimming holes.

For years the onslaught of sweeping destruction was relentless, but eventually the lumbermen moved on. The land, having been stripped bare of its natural resources, was devastated, but would now be left to rejuvenate and heal. In time, saplings grew into towering trees once again and the fast-flowing rivers eventually broke down the man-made barriers to wash away most reminders of human infringement. Logging roads eventually grew over and trees and bushes all but erased their existence.

While logging once reigned supreme in the region, in time only hunters and trackers were lured there, enticed to the new-growth forests by the rich array of wildlife known to inhabit the woods. They were pulled to the waterways on the promise of lakes and streams teeming with fish.

It took many cycles, but eventually the land returned to its natural order. Today, the region has been restored to its former natural beauty and bounty, though hunters and trappers continue to chase their game. But there is more to this large tract of land than the man-made history. In fact, the legend surrounding this mysterious piece of land can be traced back to the mid to late 1800s, if not further.

According to local legend, in the fall of 1894, three men from the community of Milton, a quaint village bordering Liverpool to the north and hugging the banks of the Mersey River, ventured into the dense wilderness that surrounds the Eagle Lake-Long Lake area. They went in search of moose, which, at that time, were plentiful throughout mainland Nova Scotia. Today, the mainland moose is an endangered species and to spot them anywhere in the province is a rare spectacle, indeed.

As the story goes, the trio were experienced hunters and trappers. All three were said to know the local woods inside and out as they each had practically grown up in the wilderness, having roamed the woods since they were youngsters. Armed with years of knowledge and experience, the three made their way up the east bank of the Mersey River, eventually making their way to a bog located between Eagle and Long Lake. They made camp there at a high vantage point that gave them a clear view of the land and kept them out of the wetland.

The first night they spent there was uneventful and by first light the men felt the conditions were perfect for moose hunting, so off they went. A low mist hung in the air and the air was deathly still as the trio tracked their quarry. One of the men, known to be an excellent moose caller, let loose the low guttural cry of a cow moose in search of a mate.

In due time, the men expected to hear a reply, but to no avail. The calls went unanswered, as they did for the entire day.

With a light breeze picking up, the men were ready to quit as they felt that after several hours with no reply, the hunt would have to wait for another day. Just as they were ready to head back to camp, a large bull moose appeared in the middle of the bog. It seemed to be floating on the mist, as if the animal was levitating.

The unsettling illusion gave all three seasoned woodsmen a terrible start, but they snapped back to attention when they saw the moose was moving away from them, obviously in search of the cow moose that it had been hearing all that morning.

Quickly aiming his .44, one of the hunters fired three shots at the moose, but they remained amazed as the animal continued moving away, unfazed by the gunshots. Minutes later, the moose meandered into a clump of trees and disappeared without a trace.

When the men went to the spot where they had seen the moose, they were surprised that there were no visible tracks on the bog floor, nor was there any blood on the ground.

It was the second point that mostly disturbed the men because these were seasoned hunters and when they aimed a gun, they seldom — if ever — missed their target. They all agreed that with three bullets being fired, there was no way they would have missed that large moose. No way!

But apparently they did. And despite searching for several more days, the trio returned home from their hunting trip empty handed. That was a rare occurrence for these men, by most accounts. However, according to the story the men told, the moose was unlike anything any of them had ever seen in all their years of hunting those historic woods. They said it was like the animal had risen spirit-like out of the mist and had mysteriously evaded the shots. How that happened, they could not explain.

Such stories of strange beasts roaming the bog around the three lakes became common as tales of encounters with an unusually large moose that seemed to be floating on the water became the stuff of local legend, passed down from one person to another until the stories gained folklore status.

In future years, the stories became more common and were further enhanced as other hunters, trappers and woodsmen not only reported seeing this storied moose, but reports of strange and blood-curdling cries and howls also began to circulate. One of those reports comes from the fall of 1896 when two local men from the nearby village made their way into the dense woods and set up camp near the bog, the same area where the three hunters had previously camped.

It was during the first day of hunting that one of the pair took his rifle and found a perch on a high elevation that would give him a clear view of the entire bog. Almost immediately, the story goes, the still morning air was shattered with a screeching sound that was so strange that it defied all descriptions. According to the man's account of the incident, the sound originated at the top of a ridge and wafted down over the bog as if blanketing the entire area, and it echoed throughout the dense woods until it finally dissipated.

The unearthly sound was so loud and piercing that it left the hunter shaken to the very bone. Never before had he heard of such a sound and when his companion, who had also heard the "scream," joined him, they agreed it was not made from anything natural. Within minutes, the sound came again, sweeping away across the bog and disappearing over Eagle Lake, leaving both shaken to their cores, agreeing that the sound was not of this world.

Returning to their campsite, the seasoned hunters tried to explain what they had heard. They were sure it was not a bear or a moose or any other animal they had ever encountered, and they had practically grown up in these woods. But if not an animal, then what could have made the eerie, unholy, shrieking noise?

Despite spending the next day searching around the bog for tracks of an animal that they could connect to the sounds, they could find nothing. In fact, despite hunting and searching the entire bog region for the next week, they never heard the noise again, nor did they encounter anything further unusual. Whatever it was that caused such a ruckus on their first day in the woods was gone, leaving behind no explanation.

However, even though they returned to the area to hunt again over future years, the men admitted that a certain wave of uneasiness always gripped them whenever they passed through what locals had now begun to call "the haunted bog" and they never made camp there again.

There is a place near the Town of Liverpool that locals call The Haunted Bog. The Mi'kmaq had their own name for the mystical place. Earlier generations called it "Indian Devil Country."

The name for this place appears to have been well placed. In the fall of 1898, as three hunters took up position on a knoll overlooking the bog, it is said that a loud moaning sound suddenly rang out of the heart of the bog. It was said to be such an agonizing, wailing and gut-wrenching sound that it led the hunters to believe that an animal, perhaps a bear, was brutalizing someone or something. The noise swept quickly along the bog and dissipated over Eagle Lake.

The men were shaken and uneasy. In later conveying their story to others, the three hunters all agreed that the sound was unlike anything they had ever heard before and all agreed they never wanted to hear it again. But what of the sound? Where could it come from? What could be making it? What of its origins?

The Mi'kmaq are Indigenous peoples who are among the original inhabitants in the Atlantic Provinces of Canada. The Mersey River was known to be one of their popular canoe routes across the province. Along the way they would set up encampments and establish small settlements. The region around the three lakes that encircle the bog was also known to be the place of several Mi'kmaw encampments.

According to the Mi'kmaw story, the bog, meadows and surrounding areas were said to be haunted by a devil, and the people referred to the region as Indian Devil Country. Down through the centuries, there are many stories of this mournful cry being heard over the bog, however, no one has ever been able to explain its origin.

It was a Mi'kmaw Elder who, passing the word on to famed Liverpool author and historian Thomas H. Raddall, may have unlocked the mystery of the haunted bog. Through his research and working with some of his Mi'kmaw acquaintances, Raddall tells a story through an Elder of how, in ancient times, there had been a large encampment of Mi'kmaq at Indian Gardens, located at the southern part of Lake Rossignol, another lake that flowed into the three other lakes mentioned earlier.

Raddall says he was told by the Elder that when a death occurred in the tribe the people would transport the body to Kempton Lake meadow where a shallow pit was dug and a platform was erected over it. The corpse was then placed on the platform and left to nature's scavengers. After a suitable waiting period, the people would return, set the platform ablaze and allow it and the skeletal remains to fall into the shallow pit. The grave would then be filled in and covered with ground to obscure it from intruders.

Does that explain the strange, blood-curdling cries that have been heard wafting through the air in that location? Perhaps, but who can say for sure?

Lest you think this is an old legend with no modern ties, think again. Even after all this time, there are many current local examples of people venturing into the woods surrounding the bog and emerging with stories of hearing strange sounds, experiencing uneasy feelings and even, in some cases, having actual run-ins with "something" they could not explain.

While many of these incidents are similar to those catalogued from the past, some of the more modern reports have added a new twist — actual physical contact. Well, sort of physical contact, if you include scratching at tents during the night as contact. Primarily, though, as with the historical accounts, the modern incidents mostly relate to unexplainable, blood curdling cries unlike anything that has ever been heard.

And those who have had these experiences are left with an indelible feeling that they had encountered something from beyond this world.

While Liverpool resident Stephen Rafuse admits he didn't hear or see anything during his first and only trip to the bog, he did have an experience there that was unlike anything he had previously encountered, or anything he's encountered since. Until this experience, he had not been aware of the legend that surrounds The Haunted Bog.

It was a warm, sunny spring day several years ago. He grabbed his fishing rod and headed into the area around Little Brook just off of Long Lake. A knowledgeable woodsman who spent many years fishing the rivers, lakes and streams around Queens County, for some reason Stephen had never before fished in those lakes, but he always wanted to try them as he had heard the waters there were teeming with trout.

He preferred to fish alone, for a better communion with nature. Armed with his fishing gear, a compass and a topographical map, he headed into the region encircled by the three lakes. Following previously established paths, Stephen made his away along the shores until he reached his destination.

The pristine nature was breathtaking, he says, pointing out that during his trek he had found old cabins and campsites where earlier hunters, trappers and fishers had obviously stopped and spent their time. He describes it as a surreal experience. He could connect with nature yet sense the history of the place.

"The camps were old and you could actually see where the bear had been pulling at the tarpaper as their claw marks were very visible. It was obvious those structures had been there for a long time. Being there was both relaxing and a bit unsettling at the same time," Stephen says, describing his feelings. "Kind of strange but exhilarating and honestly, I'd say I was experiencing a kind of mixed bag of emotions."

After spending the day, moving to various locations along the lake system and catching a number of trout, he says when the shadows started getting longer, he knew it was time to pack up and head for home.

Retracing his steps, Stephen discovered a new path near an abandoned cabin he felt was a shortcut around the lakes and back to his car. If he was right, he believed it would save him considerable time, so he followed the route.

"It wasn't long after I began walking along that path that I began to sense something," Stephen says. "I couldn't hear anything, but I could sense it and I had this strong feeling that I wasn't alone, like someone was coming up behind me, and very quickly. I actually believed that someone else was in the woods and was also following the path to get out before it turned dark."

He stopped in his tracks and quickly spun around, expecting to see someone else there. But there was no one.

"I thought that was odd, but just kind of shrugged it off and started walking again," he says. "But then I felt it again and quickly turned around. Still, there wasn't anyone there."

Even though he couldn't see anyone, Stephen says the feelings were so strong that he began to backtrack along the path expecting to run into someone.

As an experienced woodsman, he knows that sometimes being out in the wilderness one's mind can play tricks on itself. But that wasn't it.

"I had been in the woods enough to know that this was different," he says. "This feeling was the kind that gives you goosebumps."

Whatever it was that was on the path with Stephen that day left him with a feeling that he had encountered something that defied explanation, something so profound that when he returned to his car that afternoon, he left the area and has never returned to the Haunted Bog.

Strange but True
Where Evil Lurks

O f all the superstitions that have been handed down through the ages, from one generation to the next, none carry as much clout or reverence as those that warn us that evil is in our midst. The belief in signs of evil lurking has existed in various forms for centuries.

Earlier civilizations have deduced signs from the symptoms of sick people; the events or actions of a person's life; dreams and visions; the appearance of a man's shadow; from fire, flame, light or smoke; the state and condition of cities and their streets, of fields, marshes, rivers and lands. From the appearances of the stars and planets, of eclipses, meteors, shooting stars, the direction of winds, the form of clouds, thunder and lightning and other weather incidents, those who were able to interpret the signs were able to forecast events, usually of an evil nature.

Depending on one's own personal values and beliefs, there may be grounds for placing trust in certain evil omens. Some have had personal experiences witnessing horrendous events soon after ominous omens. Some hold beliefs in omens that have been influenced by others. Regardless of the source of these beliefs in omens, it is clear many people still hold them.

While it is easy to dismiss the belief in omens as superstition or following old wives tales, perhaps we should not be so quick to discount such beliefs. Researchers suggest that if we believe some omens may in fact foretell the future, such beliefs can help us accumulate a record, oral or written, of unpleasant events connected with omens, i.e. the things that tend to foretell catastrophe. In time, this knowledge becomes accepted as true and is handed down from generation to generation.

Often, with the passage of years, the stories get twisted, new meanings taken from them. Many omens are originally derived from the observation of the environment and natural phenomena.

Among the most common beliefs are those superstitions that warn of the presence of evil and there are just as many that offer ways of fending off evil. One that is most common in Nova Scotia is the belief that if you think a witch is visiting your house, you should stick a woman's hairpin in the corner of your door casings. If you do not have a hairpin, a fork or knife will work the same magic and the alleged evil will not enter.

Reports of such findings become common throughout the province as older homes are renovated. ... Strange, but true.

When Bobby Was There, but He Really Wasn't

What do you get when you take five lifelong friends who have been buddies since their high school days, and mix in an annual, three-day retreat at one of Nova Scotia's premier resorts?

Well, you get a good ole-fashioned ghost story, that's what.

Bobby, Keith, Brian, Darcy and Simon (last names withheld by request) have been best friends since they met in high school. As members of the school "B" basketball team, they were immediately drawn to each other. Despite coming from diverse childhood backgrounds, they created a bond that remained strong and true, defying the years and the many changes life threw at them.

After high school, the young men pursued their own callings, each carving out an impressive career in their respective fields — one a lawyer, one a financial investor, one an entrepreneur, one an artist and one a manager at a major supermarket. In their private lives, each of the friends found his life mate and settled down with families and large homes worthy of their stations.

They each did well for themselves, but no matter where their life paths took them, they each managed to find their way back to Nova Scotia for a reunion that became an annual tradition.

Nestled in the beautiful Cape Breton Highlands, Keltic Lodge is one of the premier destinations in Nova Scotia. Each May, the five friends would gather there for a weekend of revelry, comradeship and reminiscing. The yearly rendezvous became a must-do event for the five. And, without fail, for 16 years, the guys travelled from their homes in communities scattered across Canada and met at the Keltic Lodge for three days of partying and catching up.

When they parted ways on the Sunday of their annual reunion, each promised they would see the others the following year. Come hell or high water, they were committed to their friendship and nothing would prevent them from being there.

But as usually happens fate had other plans. As the old saying goes, "The best laid plans of mice and men often go awry."

About a month after their 16th reunion in 2014, Bobby, the entrepreneur, went for his annual medical checkup, during which time his doctor discovered an anomaly in his blood work. As a result, he was sent for further testing. Within a few weeks, Bobby was diagnosed with pancreatic cancer.

The prognosis was not good. Doctors told Bobby he should immediately get his affairs in order, as his time was short. While it is not an exact science to predict how long a terminal patient may have, Bobby's doctor told him that he had somewhere between six and eight months. By the end of November of that year, Bobby was dead. Despite a valiant effort, he had succumbed to the ravages of the dreadful disease.

The news of Bobby's passing hit his friends extremely hard. While each had suffered losses in their own lives, this was the first death in their close fellowship. Bobby's death left a massive void, a hole that the others felt they could never fill. To lose one of their brothers — someone with whom they had shared so much of their lives — was a seemingly insurmountable hill to climb. So much so that the remaining friends considered cancelling their annual reunion the coming May.

However, as Keith, Brian, Darcy and Simon gathered in December 2014 for their friend's funeral, they reminisced about all the good times they had together over the years and eventually, through their grief, they decided the reunion should go on as planned. Bobby would not want them to cancel the getaway. So, like it had for 16 years, the next reunion would proceed.

The four remaining friends gathered in May 2015 at the Keltic Lodge for a weekend of fun, fellowship and frivolity. Try as they might, though, the reunion was a somewhat morbid affair, with much of the three days being spent lamenting their lost friend and remembering the good old days when it was the five of them.

They tried to pull it together, doing the usual things like eating, drinking, swimming and relaxing, but their heart wasn't in it. They desperately missed Bobby and sadly, they felt that maybe holding the reunion so close after their friend's death wasn't such a good idea after all.

Throughout the weekend Brian, who usually documented the excursions in photographs, took dozens of photos. He promised to forward them to the others when he felt the time was right. He didn't know when that time would be, as he felt that to share those photos too soon would only serve as a painful reminder that Bobby wasn't present for any of the shots.

Or was he?

At the conclusion of the May 2015 reunion, Brian downloaded all the photos he had taken from the weekend. But, even though he often thought he should send the photos to his friends, he didn't view them again for several months.

Although we may think we will never get over the loss of a loved one, time has a way of soothing one's pain and suffering. By August of that summer, Brian and the others had pretty much come to terms that their brother, Bobby, was gone, and they had a choice. They could let his death pull apart the friendship, or they could accept the reality and move on. They chose to move on, vowing that Bobby would always be part of their fellowship, even if only in spirit.

And in spirit it was.

It had been three months since he and the others gathered at the lodge and Brian felt he was now strong enough to look at the pictures he had taken that weekend. He knew it would be difficult to look at the images because they would be a reminder that Bobby was gone, but he felt it was time.

There were only 126 images from the 2015 reunion, a far sight fewer than he had taken on previous events, but he chalked up that lack of enthusiasm for taking pictures to the grief of missing his friend. He swallowed hard and began scanning the images. That's when he saw it ... him.

There was Bobby, in three of the photos ... or at least, there was his spirit. How could that be?

He meticulously studied each of three of three photos — one taken around the fire pit, where they had gathered to drink beer on their first night at the lodge; one taken as they met in the lodge's lounge after dinner on the second night; and one taken in Darcy's room, where they had gathered for a few more after-dinner drinks and just to hang out.

The images were not clearly defined, more like a smudge or a blur, but there was no mistaking it. Brian is convinced that the image was that of Bobby.

While the image does not have a face, Brian says you can clearly see it is the shape and outline of a person that the friends are convinced is actually that of their deceased buddy, Bobby.

Had Bobby found a way to meet with his friends for one last reunion?

It would seem so.

Guess Who's Coming to Dinner

Legend has it that there are 365 islands in Mahone Bay, Nova Scotia (the body of water, not the town). Big Tancook Island is the largest of the islands. It measures approximately four kilometres (north to south) by 1.6 kilometres, forming roughly a "C" shape. The island is 550 acres (2.2 km²) in size and has a rocky shoreline with open fields and softwood forests dotted by ponds, residential properties and fish stores.

Big Tancook Island is separated from nearby Little Tancook Island to the east by a one-kilometre wide strait known as "The Chops." The nearest point of land on the mainland, Sandy Cove Point on the Aspotogan Peninsula, is approximately four kilometres away. Wildlife populations on the island are limited to deer, muskrats, snakes and pheasants, as well as a great variety of birds.

The only community located on Big Tancook Island is the settlement known as Big Tancook. It has a population of about 200 residents in summer and roughly 120 in winter. Tancook is home to one of the last two remaining one-room schoolhouses in Canada — Big Tancook Island Elementary School, which also serves Little Tancook Island. High school students take the ferry every day to the mainland town of Chester.

The island has a long history and was once a summer fishing ground for the Mi'kmaq. It is no surprise that the word "Tancook" means "facing the open sea" in Mi'kmaw, the language of the original inhabitants. When Europeans arrived in Nova Scotia, German immigrants located to Big Tancook where they established a settlement, eking out their existence mostly from the bounty of the sea.

Today, like their ancestors, those who call Tancook their home primarily make their living through fishing. There was a time when the art of making sauerkraut was a mainstay of the local economy. As the traditional industries fall on tough times, however, many have turned to tourism to earn a dollar.

With no permanent link to the mainland, a scheduled ferry service operates daily year-round, running from Chester to Big Tancook Island and Little Tancook Island. The MV *William G. Ernst* is a passenger-only ferry operated by the provincial Department of Transportation and Infrastructure Renewal. Emergency response is provided by the Big Tancook Island Emergency Response Association, which is supported through volunteer efforts and community fundraising.

That's the physical world on Big Tancook Island, but what of the spiritual world? Do ghosts and spirits roam the historical island? At least one couple — John and Cathy Elliott — say yes, without a doubt.

The Elliotts have called the island their home since they purchased the former Baptist parsonage in 2010. They say they have nearly 10 years of paranormal experiences to support their belief that the house they bought — or at least some of the furniture they have added to the home over the years — came with its own spirits.

John is a retired Toronto lawyer and bookseller. Cathy is a trained landscape architect who retired from her job in acquisitions with CIBC when she moved to Nova Scotia. They say that while they love their property and everything associated with it, such as their neighbours and the natural environment, their time on the island has opened their eyes to the paranormal world.

A view from the south showing the Elliotts' house, built in 1947 to house the ministers of the Baptist Church, which is across the road. Over the years, there were probably about 20 different ministers who lived in the house until the church was discontinued and the parsonage sold about 15 years ago.

Prior to purchasing and moving into the parsonage, which was built in 1947, neither John nor Cathy admit they held any particularly strong beliefs one way or the other about the paranormal world. They never really gave much thought to spirits, ghosts or any other such thing.

"We just never really paid that much attention to it," Cathy says. "However, after our 10 years of experiences at our house on Tancook Island, we have both had our eyes opened, to put it mildly."

In explaining how the couple ended up on the island, John says it was basically a fluke.

"We were living in Toronto and looking at retirement to some place away from the hectic city life," he says. "We had been searching the Internet for possible places to buy that would be our retirement home and Cathy discovered the house on Tancook. We checked things out and eventually we ended up buying the house, sight-unseen, in 2010."

The two-story structure, which the Elliotts bought from a California couple who had purchased the property from the Baptist Church several years earlier, has three large bedrooms, a kitchen, living room and bathroom.

"It's a beautiful property and we fell in love with it right away, even without seeing it in person," Cathy says, adding that even though they have experienced some strange phenomena over the years, they have no regrets about moving to the island.

Once the sale was complete, John and Cathy used the house as their summer getaway, coming to Tancook for two weeks each season. When they retired in 2013, they permanently relocated to the island and never looked back.

"It is a wonderful place to live," Cathy enthuses. "The people are so friendly and the views are spectacular. It's such a unique place because it's isolated. It's kind of like going back in time. It's a real paradise. Who wouldn't want to live there?"

The only issue they had with the house when they purchased it was that it was empty. Because they were not prepared to move all their furniture all the way from Toronto, they had to go looking for things for the home.

"It was fun actually," Cathy says. "But the real challenge was finding pieces of furniture on the island so that we wouldn't have to move items from the mainland. Since the ferry is the only link to Tancook, that would have been a challenge and we didn't really want to engage in that."

One of the first things they purchased on the island during their first summer there was a wooden kitchen table and the accompanying four chairs that had been in storage in the church basement.

An image of the church, which dates back to the late 1800s.

"We don't really know the history of that table and chairs or who it belonged to but it was a nice set so we bought it, cleaned it up and moved it into the kitchen, where it seemed to fit in quite well," John says, adding that since they were going back to Toronto that fall, they took lots of pictures, inside and out.

Their first brush with the paranormal came after they got back to Toronto and they were showing the pictures of the property to friends and family.

"We really hadn't looked at the photos after we took them," Cathy says, "but one of our friends quickly pointed out in some of the photos that all the chairs were covered in orbs. It was pretty weird and we really couldn't explain what that was all about. We had taken lots of photos and those orbs only appear with the table and chairs. And they weren't there when we took the photos or we would have seen them."

The Elliotts are now convinced that while they had never heard of the house itself being haunted, they believe the table and chairs were possessed, and they brought a spirit into the house with them.

It's like they invited someone — or something — to dinner and that something decided to stay ... permanently.

While the couple continued to visit the home each summer, it really wasn't until they became permanent residents in November 2013 that they really became tuned in to the paranormal activity happening there.

"When we'd go to bed at night," John says, "we could hear someone wearing heavy boots coming up the stairs, and since there was no one else in the house ... well, you know."

Cathy chuckles, "I talk to them. I went to the top of the stairs and told whoever it was that they were welcomed to live in our house just as long as they didn't bother us."

On other occasions, Cathy says she could hear children playing in another bedroom even though there were no children around.

"I could hear them jumping on the bed, like children do," she explains. "Bouncing up and down, and then I would hear their feet racing down the hall to the stairs."

The funny thing, John adds, is that the upstairs floors are carpeted but it sounded as if the footsteps were on a wooden floor.

But the strange activity didn't stop there, Cathy says.

"I read a lot," she explains. "Sometimes, when I'm

sitting on the couch reading, I can hear women talking and it's almost like they are having a quilting bee or something like that. ... They seem like they're having a really good time. I think I would enjoy spending time with them."

Both John and Cathy have also heard men laughing and talking in the house. "And they are being really loud," she adds.

Other activity they've encountered in the house include lights and lamps being turned on by themselves, water jugs being moved from the kitchen counter to inside the fridge and pieces of puzzles going missing and showing up in strange places like between the outer and inner panes of their kitchen window.

Their cats have been observed behaving "peculiar" around the staircase on many occasions.

But one particular event has left them a little "spooked" but not frightened.

"They have touched me," John says. "I've felt them. One actually pinched me on the leg and left a mark, and more than once I've heard one of them exhale directly into my ear. These two things are more than a little strange but not at all scary. We just go with it."

Regardless of this unexplained phenomena, the Elliotts say they are content, happy and feel safe in their Tancook Island home. Even though they have bought a second home up the coast in the larger town of Bridgewater, they say they have no intention of letting go of their island property and will continue to use it as their summer getaway.

"We love it there," they agree. "We plan to visit there as often as possible."

In light of this activity, the couple say they began asking around with their neighbours to see if there had ever been reports of paranormal activity in their home. Everyone agrees they have not heard of anything.

"Since 90 percent of the furniture came from around the island, I think some of the pieces came imbued with spirits," Cathy says. "That's what I believe, anyway. If not, where did they come from?"

In fact, John says, the only ghost story even remotely connected to their property is that of a local legend that says a black dog haunts the road that goes directly past the house — the former parsonage — and leads to the local cemetery.

"The story goes that people have seen the black dog on the road and then it goes to the grave of its master who is buried in the cemetery," John explains. "Once it gets there, it disappears."

Could that have something to do with the spiritual activity in their house? Neither Cathy nor John believes it does, but even though they can't answer any of the questions about who or what haunts their home, they are content to share the property.

Photo by John Elliott

The Elliotts' house taken on a clear day. The road that passes by the house is where the ghostly black dog is said to roam.

The Backseat Driver

The open road can sometimes be a lonely place, but as a regional manager for a large retail chain, Ross has been driving the highways and backroads of Nova Scotia for many years. He figures he knows every kilometre of the province's pavement by heart, almost as well as he knows the back of his hand. In fact, he jokes, he knows the roads so well that if he could set his car on automatic pilot, he's sure the vehicle would find its own way home.

For the most part, the trips are long and tedious with many kilometres of nothing but forests and rocks to keep his attention, but Ross knows if he's lucky, it's possible he might see the taillights of a vehicle in front of him, or maybe even meet a passing motorist. At least seeing the lights of another vehicle breaks up the monotony and if it's late, he finds himself wondering who else would possibly be on the road at such an ungodly hour along with him.

Who's in that vehicle, he wonders, watching the red dots punctuate the darkness in front of him? Are they alone? Where are they heading? Where did they come from? Are they going back home or leaving? What's their mission? Are they as tired as he is?

If he's alone in his vehicle and it's late at night, these trips can be extremely nerve wracking and Ross often wishes for company to keep him from falling a sleep behind the wheel. He's tried all the normal tricks to keep awake such as drinking black coffee, but that only makes him want to pee. He tries keeping his windows rolled down, even in the winter, and listening to the radio, but that can become monotonous. Sometimes he prefers the silence.

Tonight he's having an especially difficult time concentrating on the road in front of him. His eyes are heavy and his mind is wandering to places he'd rather not venture, as the yellow line attempts to lull him into a trance. On these rare occasions, he decides it's better to pull over and rest instead of pushing onward and maybe leaving the road.

"Damn," he sighs, rubbing his eyes and yawning, glancing at the green glow coming from the digital clock in the dash. Realizing that with more than an hour to go before he gets home, he doesn't think he should take the chance of further driving. Finding a long stretch of Highway 103 with clear visibility in all directions in an area near Exit 9, he pulls his car off to the shoulder of the road, puts it in park and turns off the transmission.

Fumbling in his jacket pocket for his cellphone, he quickly presses the tiny button that connects to a programmed number and watches as the small screen confirms he's phoning home.

"Hello?" It's his wife, Paula, sounding groggy. He's sure he just woke her up.

"Paula. It's Ross."

"Ross?" He can detect her immediate panic. "What's wrong?"

"Everything's fine, honey," he says, fighting to stifle the yawn that confirms this was a good decision. "I just wanted to let you know I'm going to be late getting home. Didn't want you to worry."

"What time is it?"

"It's almost midnight," he tells her. "Did I wake you?"

"It's okay," she tells him. "I had been watching television and I must have dozed off. I was trying to stay awake until you got home, but I guess I was just too tired. You know I worry about you when you're on the road all alone at this time of night. Is everything okay?"

"Yes," he sighs, stifling another yawn. "Everything is fine. Had a real busy day and now I'm just feeling a little tired. I've pulled off the road so I can close my eyes for a few minutes. I won't be along for a while. It's late. Why don't you go to bed and I'll let you know when I get home?"

"Are you sure you're okay?"

"I'm fine, honey. Like I said, just tired," he insists. "I'm going to close my eyes for a few minutes. Talk to you later, okay?"

"Okay, if you're sure."

"I am," he says. "I just need to rest for a bit."

"See you when you get home."

"Bye," he quickly replies, turning off the phone and placing it on the console. Pushing his head back on the leather headrest, he closes his eyes and immediately falls asleep.

It seems like he hasn't been sleeping more than a few minutes when he hears someone calling his name.

"Ross," the gentle voice says, bringing him back to the present. "Ross. Wake up."

"What?" Ross whispers, his eyes snapping open. He pulls his body up behind the steering wheel. "What is it?"

"Wake up Ross," he hears the man's voice tell him again.

"I'm awake," he insists, his body becoming more rigid as he glances around the interior of the car. Clearing his throat, he repeats, "I'm awake."

"Are you sure you want to stop here?" the man asks him.

"What?" Ross asks, looking around the vehicle. He knows he's alone and the fact that he can hear another person's voice is starting to freak him out.

"Are you sure this is where you want to stop?"

Quickly snapping to his senses, Ross glances into his rear-view mirror and is shocked to catch a fleeting glimpse of a man in the backseat of his car.

"What the hell?" he whispers, feeling the breath catch in his throat, so dry it feels like he hasn't had water for days.

Spinning around he expects to find someone sitting there, although he has no idea who it would be or how anyone would have gotten into his car. He's sure all the doors were locked when he dozed off.

"Who are ..."

Rubbing his eyes, he stares blankly at the empty seat. Maybe he was dreaming, he thinks, but he's pretty sure he was awake and he's convinced that even though it happened quickly, there was a man in the backseat and he had been there long enough for Ross to get a good look at him. He knows there was, indeed, a man there.

Of that, he is sure. There is no doubt, he tells himself.

He's always been proud of his ability to pay attention to even the most minute details and he's sure the passenger in the backseat was a man, middle-aged, maybe around fifty, and he was heavy-set, wearing a brown shirt. He had black hair and was sporting a thick, bushy moustache.

Jumping from the car, Ross quickly opens all four doors and inspects the vehicle, both the front and the backseat. Even though he has no idea how it could have happened, he accepts that it's possible someone might have gotten in the car with him while he was asleep, but following a thorough search, he finds nothing.

Once he's sure no one else is in the car, he locks the doors, turns on the ignition and resumes his homeward trek, now fully awake. His heart is beating so fast and the adrenaline is flowing so quickly through his veins there is no longer any chance of him falling asleep. An hour later, he pulls into his driveway.

"Home," he sighs heavily, leans back in the seat and rubs his eyes. He's still uneasy about what he had experienced back on the highway but now he's convinced the hallucination must have been the result of road fatigue and he must have been seeing things. What other explanation can there be, he tells himself, grabbing his briefcase from the backseat and making his way inside the house, being careful not to make any noise that would disturb his wife. He knows he promised her that he would wake her when he got home, but he sees no need to disturb her as she's resting comfortably, snuggled down under the covers.

"Morning dear," Paula says the next day as she greets her husband of nine years in the kitchen of their modest but comfortable bungalow. "Sorry I didn't hear you come in last night," she adds, flashing him a warm smile. "Were you late getting home?"

"Not too late," Ross tells her, kissing her gently on the forehead. "And I tried to be real quiet so that I wouldn't disturb you."

"Well," she tells him, grabbing a cup from the counter and filling it with coffee. "You succeeded," she adds, switching on the radio that's stationed on top of the fridge as she does every morning so that she can catch the local news. "Wonder what's happening in the world today?"

"Anyone travelling on Highway 103 to Halifax this morning will have to take a detour so leave yourself some extra time to get there," the announcer's voice spills from the radio speaker. *"Emergency personnel are still on the scene of a major motor vehicle accident involving a transport truck and two other vehicles. Details are still sketchy at this hour but early reports indicate the accident occurred around midnight near Exit 9. Officials tell us the road will be closed for several more hours while cleanup efforts continue and traffic analysts are brought in to examine the scene. While names have not been released, police say there are four fatalities, but information is being withheld until next of kin is notified."*

"Did he say near Exit 9?" Ross asks his wife. "Around midnight?"

"Yes," she nods. "That's what he said."

"Jesus," he sighs.

"What's wrong, honey?" She takes a seat across from him at the kitchen table. "You look like you've just seen a ghost."

"Well," he pauses. "I'm not so sure I didn't," he finally tells her.

"What do you mean?"

Pulling in a large mouthful of air, Ross then relates the events from last night.

"You must have been dreaming," Paula assures him. "Or maybe you were so tired that your mind and eyes must have been playing tricks on you."

"That must have been it," he agrees.

"Here," she says, sliding him the daily paper. "You look at the paper and I'll make you some breakfast."

"Just toast, please," he replies, unfolding the paper and spreading it on the table in front of him. "And coffee, if you don't mind," he adds, scanning the front page. "Got a long day ahead of me and the coffee will — My God."

"What's wrong?" his wife asks, grabbing the coffee pot and returning to the table to top off his cup. "You've got that look about you again. Are you sure you're okay?"

"No," he whispers, staring down at the newspaper. "No, I'm not."

"What is it?"

"This," Ross says, turning the front page for his wife to see. Pointing to a picture on the bottom of the page, he adds, "This is the man who was in the backseat of my car last night."

"What? Are you sure?"

"Positive," he nods. "I only managed to catch a glimpse of him in the mirror because he was there for just a second, but I am absolutely positive it was him."

Sitting at the table and scanning the page, she says, "Well, honey, I don't know what to tell you but there is no possible way this could be the man you saw."

"I will agree I was tired, but he is the man I saw." Nodding again, he insists, "He looked just like that guy in the picture."

"Well," she sighs heavily. "I'm afraid to tell you but if you think you saw him, then you were looking at a dead man."

Turning the page back for her husband and pointing to the story that accompanies the photo, she adds, "Says right here that police have finally laid charges in the case of a man who they allege was driving under the influence when he swerved across the centre line and into the path of an approaching vehicle that was being driven by another man — this man," she stresses, pointing to the picture.

"That's crazy," Ross tells his wife.

"Maybe, but the story says the man died at the scene while the other driver escaped with hardly a scratch."

"No way," Ross sighs. "When did all of this happen?"

"A year ago last night," Paula answers, studying her husband's reaction.

"You're kidding, aren't you?"

"Nope," she shakes her head. "Not according to this article."

"Wow," he says.

"Oh, it gets better."

"What do you mean?"

"Well," she hesitates and then continues. "Didn't you tell me you saw this guy around Exit 9?"

"I did," he nods. "And don't try to tell me this accident happened around Exit 9."

"Okay," she shrugs. "I won't tell you, but if this article is accurate that's exactly where the accident happened a year ago, and based on what they're saying on the radio this morning, it's around the same spot where that other accident happened last night."

"No way."

"Yes way," she nods. "You were lucky that you got out when you did."

"Yes …" he pauses and gulps down a mouthful of coffee. "Lucky, for sure."

The preceding story was based on actual events and was presented as told to the author. The identities of those involved were withheld at their request for privacy issues.

The Christmas Bell

For many, the idea of any type of paranormal activity is difficult to accept. For these people, the possibility that there is something beyond the normal realm of what we can see and logically explain is hard to even consider. The thought of ghosts, spirits, spectres and phantoms interacting with humans is simply not a concept that they are ready to embrace.

But what about miracles? Do they exist? Are they real? Do they happen? Can you accept that possibility?

At least one Halifax woman insists miracles are real because she experienced one more than 55 years ago and she says it was so profound that it shaped her entire life. Mary Bishop, who is now 76 (as of 2018), explains that when something happens that has that much impact on one's life, you have to believe it. Taking a deep breath as if to keep her emotions in check, Mary begins her story with the fact that she was only a young woman when she got married.

"It was 57 years ago and it was a different time then," she says, the cracks in her voice betraying her emotions. "Half a century ago, it was expected that women would marry young, settle down and start a family and I guess I fit right into that mould. But I was okay with that. Coming from a family of nine siblings, I loved children and couldn't wait to be a mother myself. I felt it's what I was meant to do."

Mary met Lewis Bishop in 1962, when she was 18 years old and working as a sales clerk in a large retail store in Halifax. The outlet is now closed, she quickly adds, but it was a hopping place in its day.

"I was a sales clerk and he worked on the trucks that delivered our stock," she explains, flashing a smile as a hint of shyness cracks her stoic facade. "We were very busy in those days, which meant the trucks were coming and going all the time. I didn't know much about him but I'd see him at least twice a week, and sometimes three or even four times a week, depending on the season. At Christmas, it was like I'd see him every day because there was a constant flow of products coming into the store. It was a busy place."

If love at first sight is a real thing, then Mary admits that's exactly what happened to her.

"He was a wonderful man," she gushes. "Very kind and courteous, understanding and gentle. I'm not sure if I ever saw him lose his temper, not even once, for as long as I knew him." She pauses and then quickly adds with a chuckle, "And of course he was very handsome, not in that Hollywood kind of way, but in that natural, outdoorsman kind of way. Very rugged and strong, with a soft side to him."

While the pair didn't know each other before they met at the department store, Mary says it wasn't long before they started talking and eventually became friends. In time, they fell in love.

"Thinking back on it," Mary says, "I'm not even really sure how it all happened. It was like one day I saw him in the stockroom unloading boxes and fell for him right away. He just swept me off my feet," she grins. "The next thing I knew I was walking down the aisle and Lewis was standing at the alter waiting for me. He was beaming from ear to ear. Come to think of it, I guess I probably was too."

Obviously, she chuckles, there was lots of dating in between, and Mary says she has vivid memories of each of those special dates.

"I remember everything we did together from the time we first met in the stockroom to our first date — a movie — to our wedding day even after all these years," she says. "But today it all seems like a dream ... a wonderful dream."

While the timeframe may seem relatively short in Mary's mind, in truth the two courted for a full year. Over that time they shared many joyous experiences that confirmed that Lewis was the man she was destined to spend the rest of her life with.

And then fate intervened.

Life, it seems, had other things in mind for Mary and Lewis.

Just a little over a year from the day they met in June 1960, Mary and Lewis were wed in July 1961.

"It was such a beautiful day," Mary recalls, smiling warmly as she brushes a tear from her eyes. "The weather was fabulous and all our friends and family were there to celebrate with us. Lewis and I were so happy. The day was everything that a young woman would want in her wedding day."

The year 1961 was a time of major change for Lewis and Mary Bishop. Not only did they get married, but Lewis took a new job with a long-haul trucking company and Mary got a promotion at the department store, being moved from the retail floor to administration, which meant she worked in the store's office.

"I loved my new job and while Lewis liked his new job as well, he didn't like the fact that it took him away from home for such long periods of time," she says, pausing to reflect on her long ago past. "But we made the most of it because the money he earned doing that job was much better than what he had been earning driving and unloading the stock trucks at the store."

Mary says their happiness wasn't motivated by money, but they had agreed that early on in their marriage they would endure such sacrifices to make more money. They planned to save enough to purchase a home in five years and start having children. At that time, Mary would quit her job so she could stay home and take care of the babies.

"It was a good plan and I just couldn't wait for it all to come together," Mary says. "After five years, we figured we would have enough money to do the things we wanted and what we wanted most was a home and children. So Lewis took the job that paid him the better money and even after we paid the bills, we still had some left over to put away toward the house. We would use my paycheque to buy groceries and other little things like that, but I always had some left over to put away as well. I figured the more we could save early on, the quicker we could get on with our dreams."

For the first few months of their marriage in 1961, everything was going according to that plan and they were preparing for their first Christmas together.

"We had moved into a small, one-bedroom apartment with a tiny kitchen and living room combination and a bathroom," she recalls, chuckling. "It was tight, there's no doubt about that, but it was all we needed. After all, it was just Lewis and I, and I was there alone most of the time as he was on the road a lot. Furthermore, the rental price was really cheap, which meant we could add more to our savings. Besides, we were simple people; we didn't need a grand apartment."

No matter the size of the apartment, Mary says the real key was to take what she had to work with and turn it into their home.

"It was comfortable and cozy," she explains. "It gave us everything we could ever need and we very happy there."

Sadly, that happiness was shattered on Christmas Eve 1961 during a major blizzard that hit the region hard. It's a date that has been forever seared in her memory.

"Lewis had been away for four days making a quick run to Montreal and was due back later in the afternoon of December 24," Mary recalls. "I remember that even though I was terribly worried about him I tried to block out everything and went about with the holiday preparations. I wanted our first Christmas together as a married couple to be as perfect as I could make it, right down to the decorations and the food."

When Mary finished work at 3:00 that afternoon, she went straight home and got busy. She had lots to do, including baking the turkey, fixing the vegetables and making the pies. Lewis loved coconut cream pie and she wanted to surprise him with a nice big one for dessert when he got home that evening.

As the snowstorm intensified on the outside, Mary kept busy inside, trying hard not to worry about her husband, who she knew was on the road somewhere between Moncton and Halifax, but by 5:30 she began to sense something wasn't right in the universe.

"All of a sudden, as I was standing over the kitchen making the filling for the coconut cream pie, I got this overwhelming sense of sadness and my chest became heavy, like I was having a hard time breathing. I had never felt anything like that before and I had no idea what was going on, but I knew something was wrong. It was really unnerving. I could feel it and I wanted to cry."

Still, she pushed on with her chores, forever mindful that her husband was running painfully late and trying really hard to fight the growing sense of foreboding that was fluttering in the pit of her stomach.

Then she was stopped suddenly in her tracks by the sound of a bell ringing. Odd, she thought, wondering where the sound may have come from. The television and radio were both turned off, so she knew the sound had not come from either of those devices.

Shrugging off the sound as nothing more than her imagination, Mary went back to work on her pie filling. Then she heard the bell again. This time she felt compelled to investigate. Quickly turning off the stove so as to prevent the filling from burning, she went to the living room, where she was sure she had heard the bell, and it rang again.

The sound was very distinct.

This time, Mary insists she heard the bell come from the Christmas tree that she and Lewis had decorated during the previous weekend before he left for Montreal.

"I heard it," she recalls. "Just as plain as day and just as clearly as I'm talking to you today."

Approaching the tree, Mary says she immediately gazed upon the tree ornament that Lewis had bought for her to celebrate their first Christmas together. A beautiful crystal bell hung near the top of the tree as a reminder of the man's love for his young bride.

"When he gave it to me on the night we decorated the tree, he promised me that he would buy me a new ornament for the tree for every Christmas that we spent together," Mary whispers, choking back her tears. "I'm still heartbroken that I only ever received one ornament from Lewis because we only had the one Christmas together."

Removing the bell from the Christmas tree and sitting in an old armchair that her parents had given Mary and Lewis when they moved into the apartment, Mary says she knew something terrible had happened.

"I knew it," she says. "I knew something had happened to Lewis. I didn't know what it was but I knew it was bad. I knew he was in a whole lot of trouble."

After that, everything became a bit of a blur.

Mary recalls that shortly after hearing the bell ring, she heard a knock at the apartment door and when she answered it, she was surprised to see her father and mother were there, covered in snow. Why had they ventured out in such a terrible storm, she asked them?

As it turned out, her parents were there because the police had contacted them and they told them there had been a terrible accident. They told Mary that the police had contacted her father because he was a retired police officer and they felt it would be better if they were the ones to come and tell her that Lewis's truck had been in a collision with a car. In order to avoid serious injuries to the occupants of the car, Lewis had swerved and took his truck over a rather steep embankment. He died at the scene.

Mary was devastated, her world turned upside down. In an instant her dreams were shattered and the man she so desperately loved would never be coming home to her. She had no idea how she would go on without him.

They say time heals all wounds — even deep ones created by a lost love. And in time, Mary pulled herself together and had a good life, complete with another deep love and a second marriage.

This bell, given to Mary by her late husband in 1961 to celebrate their first Christmas together, warned the woman of Lewis's impending death.

However, she always had a special place in her heart for Lewis, and their daughter, Louise.

You see, although Lewis died before Mary could tell him, Mary was pregnant with their daughter. She feels that somehow, deep down he knew they were going to be parents.

"I just feel that Lewis was with me that Christmas Eve and that he reached out to me through that Christmas bell as a way to let me know he was okay. I am sure of that."

And today, almost 60 years later, that bell has a special place on her Christmas tree right along with all the other special ornaments. In time, Mary says she will give the bell to Louise as a memory of her father ... a father she may never have met, but a father who loved her with all his heart.

Strange but True

Bayers Lake Mystery Walls

The Bayers Lake Mystery Walls are a series of stone structures and walls of unknown origin and uncertain age located in Halifax.

The ruins consist of walls outlining a small five-sided building and a 150-metre wall with ditches, both made with flat-surfaced ironstone slate rocks on the slope of a hill overlooking the Bayers Lake Park.

The mysterious ruins pose many unanswered questions for archaeologists and historians. The most simple and humble explanation suggests a sheep pen, but some suggest they were built for a military purpose, either a training installation or a defensive position. The walls are a protected archaeological site designated under Nova Scotia's Special Places Act.

The site is included within the historic limits of one of the nine original Dutch Village grants issued in 1762 — a 150-acre grant assigned to Johann Gotlieb Shermuller. Shermuller sold the property in 1770 and moved to Philadelphia, where he became a butcher.

The site changed hands many times after 1770. However, given its ground conditions, it is unlikely to ever have been farmed. A 1918 map depicts a building standing in approximately the location of the site steps, the only structure on the property for which there is known documentary evidence.

The mysterious walls located at Bayers Lake pose many unanswered questions for archaeologists and historians.

In October 1990, Jack McNab contacted local media regarding this site, as it was about to be cleared for the newly developed Bayers Lake Business Park. His effort helped protect the area. In 2013 the Nova Scotia Archaeology Society set up a committee called Bayer's Lake Walls Historical Site Advocacy, as a result of recent vandalism to the site.

In December 1998, a lichenologist examined the masonry of the wall and identified patterns of lichen growth that indicated that the stonework had not been disturbed since around 1798. ... Strange, but true.

The Ghost of Mrs. Smith

When talking about paranormal activity people often erroneously conclude that ghosts can be associated only with old buildings. In fact, nothing could be further from the truth as research has shown that hauntings can be associated with a person, animal, place, structure or thing.

For the purposes of this story, however, we are going to tap into the old axiom that would have us believe that most ghosts tend to haunt buildings because, in this case, that is exactly what's happening.

The oldest standing church in Liverpool, a quaint community on Nova Scotia's South Shore, is the Trinity Anglican Church, which was constructed in 1821 and 1822 by the Halifax Casket Company. The church, and the cemetery surrounding the building, are located near the town's main commercial core. They are notable for their historic significance in this once bustling privateer seaport.

For one, the church has a connection to some of the province's most important historical figures, including the legendary Enos Collins. Collins was a merchant, ship owner, banker and privateer. He was born to a merchant family on September 5, 1772 in Liverpool and was subsequently baptized in Trinity Anglican Church. Collins is noteworthy as the founder of the Halifax Banking Company, which in 1903 was merged with the Canadian Bank of Commerce. Upon his death on November 18, 1871, Collins was acclaimed as the richest man in Canada.

The Trinity Anglican Church, which was constructed in 1821 and 1822 by the Halifax Casket Company, is the oldest standing church in Liverpool. It is also said to be haunted.

Likewise, the Anglican Cemetery is of historical significance as it contains several old and rare tombstones. Additionally, the Seely vault — the only vault of its kind in Liverpool and perhaps the county — is located there and can be found right next to the church.

Captain Caleb Seely (1787-1869) and eight family members are buried in the vault, a rare occurrence in this town. Captain Seely was a well-known privateer and plays an important role in the town's history as he bought the house owned by noted Liverpool settler and diarist Simeon Perkins after Perkins died. Today, the Perkins House is the oldest house in the Nova Scotia Museum system.

In addition to all this history, it is also alleged that Trinity Anglican Church has a ghostly presence and while, as church parishioner and long-time volunteer Kathleen Stitt points out, no one knows for sure who the spirit belongs to, its presence has been felt for many years. Most notably, she says, the presence became stronger following the addition of a new section to the church in 1995 when a kitchen, general-purpose room, offices and washrooms were completed.

"There had been stories of something unusual going on at Trinity for many years. People talked about it all the time," Kathleen says. "But after the new parish hall was completed in 1995, things really started to happen and stories of unusual sounds being heard in the church and of things being moved around on their own became more common. Perhaps they disturbed something when they were building the new addition but ever since then, whatever has been happening at the church seems to have increased in intensity."

Reports of the paranormal activity have varied from person to person, but the claims mostly centred on footsteps being heard in the church when no humanly body could be connected to them. There were also reports of inanimate objects being moved from one place to another or of objects going missing and remaining missing for several days, only to turn up in locations that have been previously searched many times. Reports of organ or piano music being heard in the church by parishioners when there was no logical explanation are also common.

"We really have no idea what's going on at Trinity," Kathleen says. "But there have been too many reports of unusual activity over the years to dismiss them outright." Emphasizing the point, she adds, "There have been too many reports by credible witnesses to just shrug them off."

Despite there not being a ready explanation for the paranormal activity within the church, Kathleen adds that the real mystery is that they really have no idea who the spirit is.

"Truthfully," she explains, "we're not even sure if the spirit is male or female but we have taken to calling it Mrs. Smith because that just seems to fit the entity. ... Besides, we had to give it a name and Mrs. Smith just seemed appropriate so it has stuck and ... whatever happens in the church, everyone just accepts that it's Mrs. Smith doing her thing."

And that "thing" has included some pretty unusual activity over the years.

"For starters, we have had many, many reports of people putting down a book on a table only when they went to retrieve the book, they would discover it had been moved to a new location. ... It may not be so unusual for that to happen, except ... what if you are alone and you are sure you didn't move it?"

Strange.

"Objects moving around Trinity are not uncommon," Kathleen will acknowledge, pointing out that seems to be especially true of special, religious items.

"Trinity has a collection of five chalices and it was very common over the years that one of the chalices would always be missing," she says. "You could count on it and no one could explain where it had gone, but eventually it would turn up."

Only, she quickly adds, another one of the special goblets would immediately go missing. "It was like clockwork. One of the chalices is always lost, almost as if someone was taking it and hiding it."

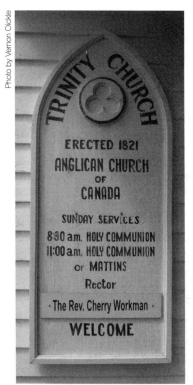

Photo by Vernon Oickle

ERECTED 1821

ANGLICAN CHURCH

OF

CANADA

SUNDAY SERVICES

8:30 a.m. HOLY COMMUNION
11:00 a.m. HOLY COMMUNION
or MATTINS

Rector

· The Rev. Cherry Workman ·

WELCOME

The church and the cemetery that surrounds the building located near the town's main commercial core are notable for their historic significance in this once bustling Privateer seaport.

Now that is strange.

You know what else is strange, Kathleen asks.

"Pieces of music that our organist would need for certain occasions would disappear," she explains. "And it would show up weeks later. These things never seem to leave the church. It's as if they just vanish and then, miraculously reappear."

Other items that have gone missing and then reappear include christening candles and keys. "They seem to be pretty popular with whoever is doing this ... or whatever."

While disappearing items are a common occurrence at Trinity Anglican Church so, too, are unexplained sounds.

"We had reports of parishioners and visitors hearing the organ playing, only it really wasn't," Kathleen points out. "The parsonage office is in the basement of the new section. We have regular reports from the parishioners of hearing someone walking around upstairs on the main floor. Only, when they went to check on who might be in there mulling around, they would find there was no one there. And, in fact, the building was empty except for the parishioner."

While the unexplained activity seems to have increased in frequency over recent decades, Kathleen says they have tried to figure out who the spirit might belong to but concedes they have no idea.

"Our best guess is that it's one of the past organists because of the musical pranks, but that's just a guess. In fact, we don't even know if it's one entity. Perhaps it's two or more."

Regardless, she says, they have just accepted the spirit as being part of the building.

"No one has ever reported being afraid or having any feelings of threats," she says. "In fact, it's just the opposite. Most people who experience Mrs. Smith report feeling at ease and comforted."

And, she adds, "Most people who spend time at Trinity will tell you they never feel alone even when there is not another person in the building."

Not another person, perhaps. But how about a soul? Perhaps a lost soul?

Could be, Kathleen agrees, but quickly adds, "You know. You never really feel alone in any church."

So true.

The Song of the Whip-poor-will

Forerunners are common in Nova Scotia folklore but what exactly is a forerunner?

A forerunner is a premonition of death. A precursor of tragedy. A warning. An omen. A foretelling or foreboding of something dark. A harbinger of evil.

There are many ways to describe a forerunner but no matter how you choose to define them, in Nova Scotia forerunners are always associated with death and anyone who has experienced such a phenomenon will agree it's unlike anything else they've encountered.

One of those people is Bill Williams. Bill, who was born and raised in Nova Scotia, relates a personal experience from a few years back that centres around the death of his sick father, Raymond. We pick up the story in August 2016.

"Dad had been sick for almost a year," Bill recalls, explaining that near the end of his life, his father had been confined to hospital with liver cancer. "It was a terrible time for everyone in the family because Dad was suffering really bad and in excruciating pain. No one wanted to see him die but it was hard seeing him like that. I couldn't stand to watch him suffer, but there was nothing they could do for him except keep him comfortable, which, I guess was all that we could ask for."

Bill, the oldest of three children in the family, had always been close to his father. He has many fond memories when, as a child, he spent quality time with his dad and recalls that he and his father enjoyed many hours traipsing all over Nova Scotia looking for birds.

"Dad was an avid birdwatcher and I remember him packing us up and heading off to different places to look for various rare species that he needed to add to his list," Bill explains. "He kept extensive and detailed records of every bird he had seen over the years including the date, time and location. He would also include details about how many were in a flock or if it was a solitary bird. He was really into that stuff and made sure I understood why it was important to keep track of birds."

The records also include intricate details of each bird, such as its colour, its size, if it appeared to be healthy or not, and whether it was a male or female member of the species.

"I really enjoyed those trips with Dad," Bill recalls. "We spent many hours together out and about in the wilderness and remote areas. We would travel from one end of the province to the other, looking for some elusive bird that Dad had heard about through his extensive network of fellow birdwatchers. Those trips became our special time and today, when I think of those times, I'm happy to have the memories."

As Bill grew older and his interests took him elsewhere, his adventures with his father became fewer and fewer until they eventually stopped altogether. But he knew his father continued to search for rare and elusive birds, all the while keeping extensive records of his journeys.

"Now, I'm very glad to have the record books," Bill says, adding that they give him a very detailed outline of his father's experiences and their earlier trips together. "Those books are very special to me. They're kind of my way of keeping him close to me."

One of the things he recalls about his father was his uncanny talent to mimic the birdcalls.

"It was amazing … really amazing," Bill says, pointing out that whenever his dad did a call it was pretty much impossible to distinguish between the real thing and the impersonation. "He had a talent, that's for sure."

Over the years, his father had perfected dozens of birdcalls but the one that he loved the most was doing the song of the whip-poor-will, a medium-sized nightjar found throughout North America. The whip-poor-will is commonly heard within its range, but is very difficult to spot because of its camouflage, which allows it to practically hide in plain sight. It is named onomatopoeically after its song.

"The way Dad could mimic that bird was simply beautiful," Bill proudly proclaims. "It was mesmerizing the way he could make that bird come to life by duplicating its song. He entertained many people with his skills and everyone was amazed. I wish I could do it but I could never get the hang of it. Dad tried to teach me many times, but I just didn't have the knack for it. Dad, on the other hand, was really a natural at it. I swear, you'd think the real bird was in the room."

It was Raymond's talent to duplicate the song of the whip-poor-will that united father and son as death was approaching and, as the emotion takes hold, Bill says he remembers the events just as if they had happened only yesterday.

"In the end, I spent as much time as I could in the hospital with Dad. Thank God I run my own business because that gave me the flexibility to come and go, as I needed to. During the last few weeks of Dad's life, I was at the hospital more than I was at the office, but I just had to be there with him. Mom had died a few years earlier and my sisters live out of the province, so it was just me and I couldn't leave him alone."

They were difficult weeks, Bill remembers, as the emotions on his face betray the raw pain that he continues to suffer to this day.

"I hated to see him like that. Even though the doctors did what they could for him, I could tell he was still suffering and it just made me feel so helpless. The only thing I could do was be with him and I was there whenever I could be."

Watching a loved one in the last days of his or her life is among the most difficult things that anyone will ever have to endure, but Bill remained by his father's side, talking to him, reading him books and simply holding his hand.

"I tried my best not to cry around him, but what can you do? When you're staring death in the face, your emotions have a way of taking over and at times, it just became too much and I had to leave, even just for a few minutes."

Near the end, Bill says he could tell that his father was slipping away and it took all his strength to sit beside the bed and watch the man that he loved fade from this world into whatever waited on the other side.

"I remember it was late in the afternoon on a Thursday in August when the nurse who was keeping watch over him came to me and told me I should go home for bit just to give myself a break. She could tell I was nearing the end of my rope. I was exhausted and emotionally drained. She suggested that an hour or so away from the hospital would do me good and she promised that if anything changed, she would call me right away so that I could come back and be with Dad."

Even though Bill felt guilty about leaving his father's side, he thought that maybe a brief reprieve might actually do him good so he agreed to go home but only after the nurse assured him that she would call at even the slightest change in his father's condition.

"Since I only live about 10 minutes from the hospital it meant I could get back quickly if Dad needed me. I went home where I found the house was empty. My wife was at work and our children were spending time with their friends so the place was quiet — too quiet. I don't like it when it's that still. It kind of gives me the creeps because you can hear everything and considering the state I was in, that wasn't a good thing."

Stopping at the kitchen counter to check the mail that had been piled there, Bill says he had just begun to make his way through the letters when, out of the blue, he heard a whip-poor-will.

"It stopped me cold in my tracks," he recalls. "I froze. I mean, I literally could not move. The cold chills ran up my back and the little hairs on my arms rose as I shook from head to toe. I had heard that song too many times not recognize it. I knew without a doubt that it was a whip-poor-will."

But how could that be? There was no one else in the house except Bill. All the radios and televisions were off. There was simply no explanation for what he had heard.

No worldly explanation, that is.

"I was dumbfounded, really. I honestly didn't know what to do and for a few seconds, I just stood there, wondering what to do next. I thought my mind must be playing tricks on me because there was simply no way I could have heard what I thought I had heard."

Then he heard the song again, for a second time.

"And this time, I knew right away what was going on," Bill says, choking back tears. "I knew it was the whip-poor-will and I knew it was Dad."

Immediately after the second birdcall, his cellphone rang and he instinctively knew what was happening.

"I knew that Dad had died before I answered the phone," Bill says with conviction. "I am convinced that Dad knew he was going to die and he waited until I left the room to do it because he didn't want me to be there when it happened. I honestly believe that he didn't want me to see him die because he thought it would be too painful for me to witness."

As to the song of the whip-poor-will, Bill says he knows what he heard that day in his house and he is 100 percent certain that it was the birdcall that his father used to make.

"I believe in my heart that Dad reached out to me as he was dying and sent that whip-poor-will song to me as a message," he insists. "I am sure that Dad was telling me that I should not worry about him because he was going to be alright and that he was no longer in any pain."

Call it a forerunner or whatever you want, but for Bill that song of the whip-poor-will was the last thing he ever received from his father and he takes comfort in the fact that while he can't logically explain what happened to him that day, he is certain that his father is doing okay and is no longer suffering.

Grandmother's Rocking Chair

Throughout the Maritimes and especially here at home in Nova Scotia, stories abound of inanimate objects being possessed by spirits. Old captain's sea chests, framed pictures, pieces of jewellery and vases all feature prominently in many local tales of the paranormal. However, one of the most common subjects of these stories is your grandmother's rocking chair. The following story, based on true events, emphasizes this reality.

"Bad day, honey?"

"The worst," the young woman sighs heavily, instinctively brushing her long, auburn-coloured hair out of her eyes. Flopping into the brown suede sofa, she kicks off her black leather pumps and wiggles her toes.

"Are you okay?"

"Yes. ... That feels so good," she whispers, her words barely audible as they slip between her taut lips. Smiling at the old woman sitting in the wooden rocking chair across from her she says, "I'm okay but I'm absolutely totally exhausted. You have no idea of the kind of day I've had, Gran."

"Oh, I think I do," the senior nods. The deep wrinkles that almost look like crevices or cracks in her face, combined with the dark purple circles under her recessed eyes, tell the story of a life journey that's been both long and, at times, rocky. "What you need, my dear, is a nice long soak in the tub," she suggests with a subtle nod and soothing smile, her words projecting the kind of comfort that only a grandmother can provide. "I always say there's nothing better than a soak in hot water to wash your troubles away."

"That's a great idea," Molly agrees, pulling her long, slender legs up under her petite frame. Tilting her head back and resting it on the floral-patterned hand-made afghan that covers the sofa, she closes her eyes tightly and sighs heavily again. "But first, I think I'll just sit here for a second and let my body unwind." Opening her eyes and winking at her grandmother, she adds, "Besides, I want to know what you did today. Do anything exciting?"

"Not likely," the old woman laughs, the cracking in her voice betraying her age. "There's not too much an old woman like me can do except to sit here in this old rocking chair and watch the outside world as it goes by, but even that's becoming difficult."

"Eyes bothering you today, Gran?" Molly looks lovingly at her grandmother and realizes just how tiny and frail the woman appears.

"Afraid so," the woman nods, rubbing her eyes with her right hand, the various-sized brown spots clearly visible on her skin and her fingers twisted and bent into hideous looking twigs that resemble the barren branches of the lilac bush just outside the living room window. It's been there for as long as Molly can remember. "I tried reading, but these tired old eyes have pretty much become useless. They've seen better days ... I can hardly focus on the page. Don't know why they have to make the type so small. Perhaps," she sighs deeply and shrugs, "I'm just getting old."

"Come on Gran," Molly replies. "You're not old."

"Really, honey? Maybe it's time that you accept the truth."

"Or maybe it's the light in here," Molly suggests, glancing around the room that's crowded full of an assortment of antique furniture, collectibles and memorabilia from her grandmother's younger life. Most of the things assembled here are reminders of earlier times when the frail woman was spry and agile; a time when this tiny old woman could work circles around other women much younger than herself. "It is kind of dingy. … I can get you another lamp if you'd like."

"I'm afraid it's not the light, honey," the old woman answers. "It's the eyes. Like I said, they've seen better days, but thank you very much for the offer."

"Come on Gran," Molly laughs. "If it's not the light, maybe it's your glasses," she suggests. "Is it time for a checkup?"

"Nope. Just had that done a few months ago and the eye doctor said there was no change from the last exam, so it's not my glasses." Studying her granddaughter, the senior quickly changes the subject. "So tell me about your day, Molly. Was it really as bad as you make it seem?"

"Oh my God, yes. It was the absolute worst," Molly nods, then rests her head back on the sofa again and closes her eyes. "It all started when I got up this morning and there was no hot water in the house. It was all downhill after that. I knew I should have gone back to bed right then and there, but Travis said he'd look after it today while I was at work so I managed to have a quick shower in cold water and then rush off to the office. I had to sit in the lineup at the service station for 15 minutes waiting to get gas because the word was out that the price was going up tomorrow morning and everyone wanted to fill up so they could save a few cents. Not me." She grits her teeth and fumes. "Isn't that just the stupidest thing you've ever heard? ... I just needed gas so I could get to the office and it makes no sense to me to sit in a long line up, burning gas, while waiting to get more gas."

"Sounds like you got off to a rough start, my dear," the old woman agrees. "I certainly hope things got better for you after that."

"You'd hope so, but they didn't," Molly replies. "If anything, they got worse. Seriously, if I had known all things, I would have turned around right then and there, and gone back home. To say all this was a bad omen might have been an understatement."

"Now come on honey," her grandmother says, her voice as soft and soothing as it's always been. Molly has always appreciated her grandmother's gentle disposition and positive outlook on life. She's helped her through some tough times over the years and Molly wonders what she would ever do without the woman in her life. She thinks she'd go insane. "No matter how bad things seem in the moment, they can always get worse."

"That they can, Gran," Molly nods. "That they can."

"So then what happened next, honey?"

"By the time I got to work, 15 minutes later than I should have, Mr. Randolph — he's my boss — was waiting to see me in his office," Molly continues. "I knew right away that wasn't good. Whenever your boss is waiting to see you and you show up late, that doesn't bode well for your future, but thankfully he didn't seem to be mad at me about any of that. Instead, he told me we had a new client coming in this morning and he wanted me to take the case. It was a botched robbery that resulted in a young boy, 15 years old, being charged. He pointed out the case could be very controversial and might even lead to a lawsuit against the town, which could result in big bucks for the firm. Mr. Randolph then promptly handed me the file and left, telling me the client would be there in about half an hour."

"That's not a bad thing, is it?" the old woman smiles. "It shows he has faith in you, doesn't it?"

"I guess so," Molly shrugs. "But I knew nothing about this client and only had a little time to become acquainted with the case so here I am rushing back to my office with the file in one hand and a cup of coffee in the other when …"

"Wait," her grandmother interrupts. "Don't tell me."

"Yes! You know it," Molly sighs. "I ran right smack-dab into another lawyer and spilled the entire cup of hot coffee all down over the front of my blouse. I was a mess."

"Oh no. What did you do?"

"The only thing I could do," Molly says, figuratively waving her hands in the air in a sign of disgust. "I rushed into the bathroom and tried to wipe off the coffee before it could have a chance to set, but you know how badly that stuff stains, especially on white cotton."

"It can be nasty," her grandmother nods. "Did you get it out?"

"Most of it, but now my blouse was soaked and the client was due any minute." Molly pauses and gathers her thoughts. "Thank God I remembered that one of the other lawyers always kept a spare blouse in her office — something I'm going to start doing from now on — so I quickly ran and borrowed that. It didn't really match my skirt, but by this time, I didn't really care. Just as long as it didn't have coffee down over the front and as long as it wasn't wet."

"So things worked out for you in the end."

"I guess," Molly agrees, expelling a loud burst of air from her lungs. "At least I had a clean blouse that was dry, so that was a good thing. After that, I rushed back to the office and tried to review the file in preparation for the client's arrival. I just get settled down behind my desk when the phone rings. . . . It was Travis and he's got bad news."

"Now what?"

"Well, he said the reason we didn't have any hot water this morning was because the hot-water tank was shot and we need a new one, which wouldn't be too bad, I guess, considering the one we had was there when we bought the house four years ago," Molly explains. "But there's another problem in that Travis said he called a plumber but they're so busy that it could be three or four days before we can get someone to come out and install the new tank. He called around town to a couple other plumbers and got the same response as the first one. ... I can't imagine what it will be like to go that long without hot water in the house."

"When I was your age, honey, there was no such thing as running hot water." The old woman laughs. "If anything, we were lucky that we had an outhouse. If that's the worst thing you have to worry about these days, my dear, then consider yourself very lucky."

"I know, Gran," Molly sighs. "My generation is really spoiled, there's no argument about that, but once you get used to something, it's not easy to adapt to not having it."

"You'll survive."

"I guess so."

"You will," the old woman assures her. "So tell me about this client. How did things go when he finally showed up?"

"I wish I could say that it went well, but like everything else today, it didn't. It was like everything I touched turned to crap." She takes a deep breath. "The kid arrived with his parents before I had a chance to completely review the file and I could tell they were not impressed that I wasn't prepared. I could have told them that I had just been handed the case, but that would not have been professional."

"Perhaps you should have told them," the old woman suggests. "It's always best to be honest, Molly. You've been taught that lesson ever since you were born. Honesty is the best policy."

"Yes," Molly nods. "But I could never do that. Trying to blame someone else makes you look incompetent."

"But it was someone else's fault, wasn't it?"

"It was, but I managed to get through it," Molly says, letting her pride shine through for just a minute. "Admittedly, I had to bluff along the way, but I think I convinced them we were the best firm to handle his case."

"So something went well for you after all."

"I guess," Molly agrees. "But we'll see on Thursday when I have another meeting with them. If I don't get them to sign with us at that time, then I'm sure there will be hell to pay. My boss made it very clear that he expected me to sign the client this morning, but I just couldn't close the deal."

"You will, dear.

"I wish I could be as sure as you about that, but after everything else that happened today, I'm not really convinced of anything."

"You're better than that," the old woman says. "You've got to have faith in yourself."

"Of course." Molly smiles. "You're right."

"So what else happened today?"

"You name it," she replies, "and it happened. It was just one of those days when everything I touched just seemed to turn to crap. After the client left I had to rush off to court for another case I'm working on and that's where I crossed swords with a prosecutor who seems more interested in making a name for herself than seeing that justice is served. The bitch."

"Molly! Language."

"Sorry, Gran. But that's what she is. She could care less that her intentions to put a teenage boy behind bars could ruin the kid's whole life. All she cares about is adding another notch to her belt, but I think there's more to this kid than she gives him credit for. We all make mistakes and I really think this guy deserves a second chance."

"Convince her."

"It's not that easy," Molly confesses. "But I'll give it my best shot, for the sake of the boy."

"I am sure you will," the old woman says, her grandmother's words oozing confidence. "I am not aware of all the details of the case but I am confident the boy is fortunate to have you in his corner. You'll help him as best you can."

"Gran," Molly blushes. "I wish I had as much confidence in myself as you have in me."

"You should, honey," her grandmother assures her. "You're a good lawyer. Besides that, you're also a good person."

"Being a good person doesn't always cut it, especially in my line of work," Molly replies. She shrugs. "But I'll do my best."

"I'm sure you will. You always do and that's all anyone can ask for," the old woman smiles. "What happened after court?"

"Everything," Molly says. "I was running late and didn't have time for lunch and I was starving by around 3:00 so I choked down a bag of chips on my way to another meeting."

"That's not healthy," her grandmother warns. "You've got to take better care of yourself or you'll get run down and then you'll get sick. Haven't we had enough sickness in the family lately?"

"Yes Gran. I know, but I just didn't have time to eat a proper lunch."

"You have to make time, young lady." Her grandmother always calls her *young lady* when she's trying to make an important point. "If you don't look out for yourself, who else will?"

"Okay," Molly sighs as the sound of her mother doing dishes in the kitchen grabs her attention. "I get it, but that wasn't the worst of it. I drove all the way over to the other side of town only to find out when I got there that my meeting had been postponed until tomorrow and no one bothered to tell me, which means I now have a scheduling problem tomorrow because I've got to be in two places at once and they're both important meetings."

"Molly," her grandmother cautions. "I'm worried about you. This stress is not good for you. You have got to slow down."

"You're telling me. Driving back to my office and fuming about having just wasted an hour of my time — an hour I didn't have to waste — I managed to run over and kill a goddamned cat."

"Molly, what did I just tell you about your language?"

"Sorry again, Gran, but the bloody thing just came out of nowhere and darted across the street," she continues. "It was awful. I can still hear the thud. It made my stomach churn — stills does when I think about it."

"Then don't think about it."

"It's hard not to. All I could do was pull over to the side of the road and sit there and cry. It was just so sad."

"What did you do about it?"

"Well, after I managed to calm myself down, I knocked on a couple of doors in the neighbourhood and on the fourth try, I managed to find the cat's owner."

"And?"

"And let's just say the woman was not happy that I had killed her cat. It didn't matter to her that the animal had run out into the street in a place where I couldn't see it. All that mattered to her was that the cat was dead." Molly wipes the tears from her eyes. "She didn't want to listen to reason. It was all my fault and that was the bottom line, so I gave her my card and told her to send me the vet's bill for the cost of disposing the poor thing."

"Was she okay with that?"

"Don't think so," Molly says. "But honestly, I didn't stick around long enough to discuss it any further with her. I could tell she was very distraught and would not listen to reason, so I got out of there as quickly as I could."

"That was probably smart."

"Yes," she nods. "I think so. God knows what that will cost me in the end."

"How did things go after that?"

"Surprisingly, the rest of the afternoon was uneventful," Molly says. "When I finally got back to the office, the place was pretty much empty so I sequestered myself in my office for about an hour and a half and worked on some files. Finally, I thought, some relief, but then when I was ready to leave I couldn't find my freaking car keys. I tore my office apart and looked everywhere for the damned things but for the life of me, I couldn't remember where in the hell I had put them."

"Obviously, since you're here now, you found them," her grandmother observes with a sly wink. "Where were they?"

"At the bottom of my freaking purse right where I threw them," she laughs, her smile lighting up the room. "The same place I had looked a thousand times but sometimes I don't think I could see the nose on my face even though it's right in front of me."

"Well," the old woman laughs. "I'm just glad you found them dear and that you were able to stop by for a visit."

"You know I'll always find a way to visit with you, Gran," Molly smiles. "Nothing will ever keep me from seeing you. You're just too important to me."

"Molly," a voice calls from the kitchen. It's Molly's mother, who has been washing the dishes and packing boxes. "Who are you talking to, honey? Are you talking to me?"

"No Mom," Molly calls back.

"Well," her mother continues, casually strolling into the spacious living room and wiping her hands on a tea towel, "you're talking to someone. I could hear you all the way out into the kitchen. You've been having a great conversation in here."

"It's Gran," Molly shrugs. "I'm talking to Gran."

The middle-aged woman stops in her tracks and studies her daughter. Finally, her voice soft and dry, she says, "You know that's not possible, don't you Molly?"

"Yes," Molly nods, "it is."

"Molly, honey," her mother continues, concerned that her daughter may finally be losing her grip on reality. "You know your grandmother died a month ago. Don't you remember?"

"Are you sure?" Molly asks.

"Yes, honey. I'm . . ." her mother answers while glancing quickly at the wooden rocking chair that had been the old woman's favourite place to sit. Her voice slowly tailing off as she observes the chair moving as if being rocked by an occupant. "... sure."

The Spirits of Randall House

According to historical records, Randall House is a late-18th-century, two-and-one-half story, wooden Georgian-style farmhouse located in Wolfville. With its colourful exterior and central location on the corner of Main Street and Victoria Avenue, the home is a prominent fixture of the town.

The house, which has retained its New England colonial character, is situated on a hill overlooking what used to be Wolfville's bustling harbour, and to the west of what was once Mud Creek, which is now Willow Park.

According to the Canadian Register of Historic Places, Randall House is valued as a provincial heritage property for its role as a landmark on one of Wolfville's main streets; its historic associations; its transformation from run-down dwelling to attractive residence and its use as a museum and community gathering place.

"The construction date of Randall House is unclear. The property changed hands nine times between 1761 and 1780, which was not uncommon as people in the Horton Township frequently traded lots to consolidate their property," the registry says.

Beginning in 1769, the deeds to the Randall House property mention a dwelling. However, it is unclear if the dwelling is Randall House. In 1780, Thomas Caldwell of Horton purchased the land. In February 1786, he sold the property and its buildings, which included a dwelling, barn, and outhouses, to Halifax merchants Thomas, James and William Cochrane. It is most likely during this period of ownership that Randall House was constructed.

Due to economic ebbs and flows, the property exchanged hands many times over the following year. Between 1808 and 1812, it was owned by Aaron Cleveland, a cooper who established his trade on the property. The lot's location in the commercial centre of Horton Township would have been an excellent spot for business.

According to the Canadian Register of Historic Places, Randall House is valued as a provincial heritage property for its role as a landmark on one of Wolfville's main streets. It's also said to be haunted.

Charles Randall purchased the house in 1812 and the property stayed in his family for 115 years. However, by 1927, the years had taken their toll on the house, which was in such poor condition it had become virtually uninhabitable.

Charles Patriquin, a retired farmer, bought the property in 1927 and with the support of his wife and family repaired the neglected building and transformed its tangled, unkempt yard into a robust vegetable garden that became a local attraction.

According to the registry, Patriquin was often seen pushing a wheelbarrow laden with fresh vegetables from his garden to the Wolfville grocery store. He also maintained a duck pond just below the slope of his garden where local children spent many happy hours. In 1947, he sold the house to the Wolfville Historical Society and in May 1949 it became the town's museum.

In its current role as a museum, Randall House chronicles the everyday lives of people living in the Wolfville area at different historical periods and from all classes of society.

And, according to several witnesses who experienced a host of unexplained phenomena over the years, the heritage house is also haunted.

Krystal Tanner is the curator and manager of Randall House. She has worked at the museum since 2014 and, like many others, she has seen and experienced many things in the historical house that defy any logical explanation — things that have led her to conclude that the place is, indeed, haunted.

"I'm sure of it," she says without hesitation. "I've had too many things happen to me in that house that you'll never convince me it isn't haunted. There is definitely something going on in here and I'm not the only one who thinks so."

She explains that during her first year working at the house, everything seemed normal, but it was really in the second year that she noticed strange things happening. At first, she admits, it kind of freaked her out a bit, but these days she just shrugs it off and takes everything in stride.

For starters, she explains, her cell phone does weird things when she's anywhere near the house.

"It's really the only place that I've noticed anything unusual with the phone," Krystal says, pointing out that her phone stops working the minute she walks into the house and starts working the minute she leaves.

"The weird thing about that is that I've asked a lot people about their phone behaviour and it seems that everyone else's phones continue to work just fine in the house," she says. "But mine just goes on the fritz and it works just fine everywhere else I go. Why is that?"

It's not just her phone that acts up, Krystal points out, adding that light bulbs throughout the house come on and off, even with the light switches turned off.

"How do they do that?" she asks. "I've had friends in the house who have also witnessed this phenomena. Lights just don't go on and off all by themselves. They just don't."

And then there are the disembodied voices that she and other people have heard in the house, voices from people who aren't there.

"In particular," Krystal continues, "we've heard a child's voice inside and outside the house when we know there are no children around. When you go looking for the child, you can't find one because he or she just isn't there."

Krystal says she often senses that she isn't alone when she is in the building working by herself.

"I'm sure everyone has had that feeling that you're not alone," she adds. "Well, I get that feeling a lot when I'm at Randall House and usually I get the feeling that I'm in the presence of a female spirit. It's a really strong feeling that someone — a woman — is with me, but I have no idea who it could be."

She is convinced the spirit is a woman just by the things it does.

"In the dining room, for example, the cupboard doors will open on their own and the china is often moved around," Krystal says, while adding that she's not saying a man wouldn't do such a thing, but she believes those actions are more in keeping with a woman.

She's also heard knocking throughout the house, knocking on doors and even on the walls, but the one thing that really sets her nerves tingling is hearing someone knocking on the mantel in the main sitting room or parlour.

"I've heard that knocking many times," she says. "But I'm not really sure why someone would knock on the mantel unless it has something to do with the fact that in earlier times, when someone died, they would often rest in repose in the parlour. I'm not saying that's connected, but it does make me wonder."

And then there are the footsteps.

"I've heard them on the stairs and others have heard them on the stairs," Krystal says. "We've also heard them on the second floor but when you go to check things out, you can never find anyone or anything that would account for the footsteps. Clearly, though, you can hear someone walking around."

Randall House is an old property, Krystal agrees, and as such she says it is normal that one should expect to hear sounds coming from the house.

"Every old house will have creaks and groans but not like these sounds," she says. "What you hear in Randall House is anything but normal."

And then there are the ghosts themselves.

While Krystal says she understands that some people have a problem accepting that ghosts really exist, she knows of at least two instances that have occurred at Randall House that prove to her that ghosts are real.

First, she explains, these spirits were seen on the second floor in what they refer to as the textile room.

"It's always cold in that room," Krystal points out. "You can't get it to warm up. The first spirit I've heard about in that room was that of an older woman sitting at a sewing machine."

Unlike another ghost that has been reported in this particular room, the woman appeared to be rather docile, as she seemed to be inspecting the sewing machine or working there.

But the second ghost was, according to Krystal, a little more spirited.

"I have a friend who insists that she was chased out of the room by a dark figure of a man and I believe her," she says. "This friend has no reason to lie about that and she was genuinely afraid of something so I'm convinced that she encountered a spirit in the room."

The spirits of Randall House are real, Krystal says, pointing out that they have had several paranormal groups conduct investigations at the property.

"They found things," she says. "For instance, during one of the investigations they've heard a woman say 'I'll come back.' It's pretty clear. You can hear the voice and the words. There is no denying what this woman is saying."

Who is this woman? No one knows for sure but Krystal points out that during other investigations they've heard names of women including "Eden" and "Sarah."

While the Eden remains a mystery as to its relationship to Randall House, the name Sarah could be more closely connected.

The wife of Charles Randall, who purchased the house in 1812, was named Sarah.

Likewise, the wife of Charles Patriquin, a retired farmer, who bought the property in 1927, was also named Sarah.

Could either of these woman be the Sarah whose name was heard during the paranormal investigations?

It's possible and the sad thing about Charles and Sarah Randall's connection to the house is that they had a child, a son, who died in the house. And then, 18 months after her baby's death, Sarah Randall died.

Interesting, you say? It sure is, but might that explain some of the paranormal activity connected to the property?

And Krystal says it's that sort of tragedy that convinced her there are spirits in Randall House. Of that, she is 100 percent certain.

Double Alex at Sambro Island

The massive stone tower on Sambro Island has stood guard at the approaches to Halifax Harbour since the city was a fledgling nine years old. It stands to reason, considering the history surrounding this structure, that there might also be the odd ghost or two roaming the property.

Chris Mills, a noted historian and a well-regarded authority on Nova Scotia lighthouses, explains that construction on the Sambro Island lighthouse was started in 1758 with workers completing the granite structure two years later.

It was a tough slog, Chris says, explaining that the men hauled the heavy granite blocks to the top of the island to lay the bottom layers of the tower, which are almost two metres thick. They completed the masonry by late 1758 and in April of the next year Captain Joseph Rous became the light's first keeper.

Early oils used for illumination weren't reliable and there were numerous complaints that if the light happened to go out, the keeper would often let the tower stay dark, especially if there weren't any ships in sight.

This didn't go down well with naval authorities in Halifax, who noted that the fatal loss of the sloop *Granby* on the Sambro Ledges in 1771 occurred "… for a want of light being kept in the lighthouse, for it is most notoriously and shamefully so, the King's ships bound into Halifax are frequently, nay, almost constantly obliged to *fire* at the lighthouse to make them show a light…!"

Better lights installed in 1772 helped the situation, Chris explains, and for the ensuing 216 years, diligent keepers kept the light burning. When necessary, they sounded all manner of fog signals from cannon to whistle to explosive charge to diaphone and, finally, a solar-powered electronic horn. In a case of perverse irony (considering the early complaints from ship owners looking for a light), complaints from a local resident helped put an *end* to the horn a few years ago.

But Sambro Light has its friends too. Years of lobbying by the Sambro Island Heritage Society led to the restoration of the stalwart tower, inside and out, in 2016. Sambro Light continues to mark the dangerous Sambro Ledges and light "the sea road to Halifax."

Today, the Sambro Island Lighthouse is the oldest surviving lighthouse in North America and as such its heritage value cannot be denied. But, history aside, the lighthouse also has value in the province's paranormal world as, over the decades, many spiritual happenings have been reported there.

One of the more popular ghosts reported on Sambro Island is known as Double Alex, the 19th-century ghost named after a British soldier, Alex Alexander.

According to local stories — some of which can be backed up by facts and some of which are best described as legend — in the early 1800s, British warships would fire their cannons to remind the lighthouse keeper they needed more light to guide them through the treacherous, rock-filled waters and into safety.

Photo by Chris Mills

Today, the Sambro Island Lighthouse is the oldest surviving lighthouse in North America and as such, its heritage value cannot be denied. But, history aside, the lighthouse also has value in the province's paranormal world as, over the decades, many spiritual happenings have been reported there.

This continued for decades until the problem of the insufficient light was solved in 1833 when several artillerymen were stationed on Sambro, where the army had installed a signal. From that vantage point, the soldiers would fire cannons to assist the ships coming into Halifax harbour. One of the artillerymen stationed there was none other than quartermaster sergeant Alex Alexander.

Now, according to legend, Alex Alexander liked his rum and was known to often visit the drinking establishments throughout the young city, where he was said to stay for hours, sometime days, drinking his cares away. This was especially easy for him to do, as it seems that whenever the unit on Sambro Island needed supplies, they would most often deployed Alex to fetch them.

You might say that was a huge mistake. On one of those excursions, Alex shrugged off his duties and went on a week-long bender during which it was said he was drunk for the entire seven days.

When the authorities finally caught up with Alex, they discovered that he had spent all of the money with which he was supposed to purchase supplies for the post on Sambro. While he may have had a good time for the week, his pleasures were abruptly curtailed when he was arrested and taken back to the island and thrown into a jail cell.

While in jail, overcome with the embarrassment of having let down his fellow soldiers, combined with dealing with alcohol withdrawal, it is said that Alex tied a noose around his neck and attempted to hang himself. However, before he could take his last breath, guards found him dangling in the air and quickly cut him down.

But it was too late. Alex subsequently succumbed to his self-inflicted injuries. He was immediately buried in shame in an unmarked grave somewhere on the island, his memory, just like his human remains, all but fading to the dust of time.

No one knows for sure where Alex Alexander — or Double Alex — was buried, but over the past century there have been numerous stories of witnesses who claim to have seen the ghost of a British soldier roaming the Sambro Island.

Could the ghost be the restless spirit of Double Alex? Perhaps, but it appears that he isn't alone as other ghostly encounters have been reported on the island for many years. Sightings of strange lights on the island have been reported for many decades.

Over the years, witnesses have claimed to have seen people standing on the rocks of Sambro Island when, upon further investigation, no one could be found there. The true identity of whoever roams the island may never be known, those names remaining hidden behind the shroud of the paranormal.

Strange but True
Dimes from Heaven

T here is a common superstition in the Maritimes stating that if you find a dime somewhere a dime ought not to be, then you have just received a message from a loved one who has gone onto Heaven. Whether or not others believe in such superstitions is of little consequence to those grieving the loss of a loved one. For those who believe, they take comfort in such discoveries.

Such was the case for a young Newfoundland woman who, several years ago, was staying at White Point Resort, about 10 minutes from Liverpool. By way of backstory, I will point out that throughout the summer months I have been telling ghost stories at the lodge every Thursday evening for several years running. Most nights, we gather around a fire on the beach, but on rainy nights we relocate to one of the nearby buildings. That is the setting for this particular incident.

During my sessions, I always invite people in the audience to share any paranormal experiences they may have had over the years. When this young woman asked if I knew anything about the Dimes from Heaven superstition, I shared what I knew and recounted a few stories I had heard over the years. As she spoke, the woman became visibly distraught, her emotions clearly getting the best of her. The pain of losing a loved was still fresh in her heart.

She told the audience that when she was young, she had been extremely close to her grandmother. In fact, she felt, between herself and her two siblings, she and her grandmother had the tightest bond. However, she became confused and upset when, after her grandmother's passing, her sisters began finding dimes in most unusual places, discoveries the family interpreted as the deceased woman reaching out to them from Heaven.

There is a common superstition in the Maritimes stating that if you find a dime somewhere a dime ought not to be, then you have just received a message from a loved one who has gone onto Heaven.

Now the upsetting part of this story was that, despite the close bond she felt she had with her grandmother, she never found any dimes, which, in her thinking, meant her grandmother was not reaching out to her. It was painfully obvious that this thought upset her a great deal.

While I was touched by this woman's story, I told her I could not explain why her grandmother may be reaching out to her siblings but not to her. If she was looking for answers, they might be difficult to find.

As we turned up the lights that evening, once the session had concluded, the woman from Newfoundland expelled a loud gasp; her emotions rushing back to the surface, tears streaking down her face. As she bent down to retrieve the purse she had placed under her chair at the beginning of the session, she found two bright and shining dimes on the floor.

She was certain that the coins were not there when we started the evening, but there they were for all to see. … Strange, but true.

Please note the preceding story is a true account as witnessed by the author. I do not usually inject myself into these stories, but in this rare case, I have made an exception.

The Power of Two

Research has proven that twins have a special sibling bond that appears unique to their genetic make up. Call it a sixth sense if you will or a special intuition between two people who have literally known each since conception, but there are many examples from around the world where twins have known when their counterpart was in trouble or in danger.

Meet Jenny and John. Their names are being protected for privacy issues. They grew up near Halifax and as far their childhood goes, Jenny says it was pretty typical with loving parents who provided them with everything they needed to grow into successful and prosperous adults.

"We had no complaints. Our parents were very supportive and loving," Jenny says, adding that no matter what she or her twin brother wanted or needed, their parents were there to help them. "We could not have asked for any better parents. They were always there for us, 100 percent."

Jenny and John are fraternal twins, born two months premature. Jenny is the oldest by almost 11 minutes and maybe that's why she's always felt the need to protect her "younger" brother.

"I know it sounds crazy," Jenny says with a slight shrug. "But ever since I can remember, I've always felt that it was my responsibility to look out for him, to take care of him. I swear that even when we were still really young babies, I felt this sort of compulsion to be his protector. It's weird, I know, but I can remember as far back to when we were two or three and just learning to get around on our own. I would hold onto him so he wouldn't fall and hurt himself."

That's how strong their bond was.

"There are just so many memories of me coming to Johnny's assistance, that sometimes it's hard for me to separate things that really happened from things that I think really happened," she recalls, pausing as to gather her thoughts and then continuing.

"That's because he was one of those kids that seemed like he was always getting into trouble of some kind. Either he was falling and getting hurt, or he was wandering away to play with other kids or he was fighting with other kids. He was just so curious that Mom always said you couldn't take your eyes off of him for a second or he would be gone off exploring on another new adventure."

She chuckles and wipes her eyes, "I remember that he did that a lot."

And no matter what John did, Jenny always knew about it.

"Even when I wasn't right there with him, I knew when Johnny was in trouble," she says, explaining that it was like she had a special "feeling" that came over her whenever her brother needed her help.

"I just knew it," she insists matter-of-factly. "I just felt it whenever he needed me, no matter how far apart we were."

The first time Jenny remembers that strong feeling was when they were four years old. She was playing in the house with her dolls but it was a warm spring day and her brother wanted to play outside.

"He was just one of those kids who had to explore and was constantly climbing around and tripping and falling," Jenny says. "Well on this day, Mom let him play in the backyard. It was fenced off so there was no danger of him running away, but he wasn't outside very long before I knew he was in trouble."

Jenny says it was a strange sensation but she can recall it just as if it happened yesterday.

"I was in my room playing when all of a sudden I just had this feeling that Johnny had hurt himself," she recalls. "It was kind of like a picture flashed in front of my eyes and I could see blood. The feeling was so strong that I went and told Mom that Johnny was hurt. She quickly ran into the backyard and there he was, sitting on the ground holding onto his left knee. It seems he was trying to climb one of the big oak trees out back and slipped. The cut was bleeding pretty hard so off to the hospital we went. Three hours later, we came home with four stitches in Johnny's knee."

From that day forward, Jenny says she knew whenever her brother did something to himself and was in pain.

"I could feel it and most of the time I would call him and ask what he had done," Jenny says. She pauses and swallows, then takes a deep breath and continues. "He'd always laugh and say, 'I was expecting your call, Sis.' And he'd always chastise me for worrying too much about him. I'd always tell him that someone had to watch out for him."

If John shared his sister's intuitive powers, he never shared that secret with her.

"Every now and then, he would just kind of shrug and tell me he didn't get it, that he didn't understand how I did that," Jenny says. "But there were times when I think he knew I was in trouble but didn't want to admit it because admitting that to me would be like admitting that we were connected in a special kind of way that most people would think was strange."

But Jenny says she didn't care what other people thought or even if they believed her.

"I knew what I could do and that's really all that matters to me," she adds.

The special bond remained strong throughout their young lives, through school and into their adult lives. Even large distances couldn't break their unique connection.

"I stayed back here in Nova Scotia but Johnny moved to BC just as soon as he finished high school," Jenny says. "He was an adventurer. I knew he would never be content to stay at home. He had the wandering bug. He was one of those people who had to get out in the big world and spread his wings. That was fine, but I missed him a lot after he moved."

The twins were 24 when their special bond was stretched to the breaking point and even to this day (in 2018), Jenny says she feels the connection remains strong, despite the fact that John has been deceased for seven years.

Describing the day her brother died, Jenny says it was the worst period of her life but she was expecting something to happen.

"I knew for several days that Johnny was in trouble because every time I would think of him, it felt like a large, black storm cloud was rolling in," she says, recalling that day in July 2011 when her brother was killed in a horrific traffic accident. "The feeling was so strong that I couldn't shake it and I couldn't even sleep for several nights because I just couldn't shake that God-awful feeling."

It wasn't like the typical "flashes" that Jenny had been experiencing throughout her entire life whenever her twin was injured or in danger. Instead, she says it was more an "image" of John in a twisted car wreck with lots of shattered glass and blood everywhere.

"I know now that it was a premonition of Johnny's accident," she says. "I tried to warn my brother that something was wrong and that something terrible was going to happen to him. I called him every day to tell him to be careful and, just like he always did when we were growing up, he just brushed me off and told me I was being paranoid or crazy."

But, Jenny adds, "I wasn't just being paranoid. I was actually seeing my brother's death days before it happened."

The events of that fateful day are forever ingrained in her memory.

"I was at work and I remember I had this terrible, pounding headache that I just couldn't shake. I know now that it was probably brought on from the stress of worrying over my brother," Jenny says. "I was working in my little cubicle when the shift manager came to me and said I had a phone call. We can't take personal calls at our desks so I knew right away that something was really wrong for the manager to come and get me."

And besides, she adds, "I could tell by looking at my manager's face that whatever was going on it was something really bad."

After that, Jenny says, everything is kind of a blur. She remembers going to her manager's office where she could take the call in private and she remembers her manger closing the office door, leaving her alone. She eventually learned that the caller had already told her manager what was wrong.

It would be an understatement to say Jenny was surprised when she answered the phone and Tanya, her brother's girlfriend, was on the other end.

"And she was crying," Jenny whispers. "No, actually, it was more like she was sobbing. She's a nice girl and I really like her. I thought Johnny was really lucky to have met her after he moved to BC. They had lived together for almost three years and I thought they'd actually get married some day."

The conversation between Jenny and Tanya was an emotional one, Jenny remembers.

"Through her tears she told me that John had been in a terrible car accident that morning on his way to work and had died when he was hit head-on by another car. Two people in the second vehicle were also killed that day."

While Jenny says her heart broke into a thousand pieces when she heard the news, she admits she really wasn't surprised.

"Call it what you want, but I knew Johnny was going to die," she says. "I sensed it. We had a special bond and I knew he was going to die. You don't have to believe it, but it's true; it really happened."

Today, when Jenny thinks of her twin brother she is reminded of those warnings that she had been receiving for several days before the accident.

"I can't stop wondering, 'if he had only listened to me. What if he had paid attention to my premonitions instead of dismissing my feelings as silly paranoia?'" she says. "Maybe, if I could have convinced him to stay at home for that day or to take a different route, he would be alive today, but he would not admit that maybe I was onto something. He would never believe that."

Today, Jenny says it's difficult to accept that her twin brother is gone.

"He is part of me," she says. "I miss him so much and think about him every day. At times I can still feel him. Call me crazy if you want to, but I believe he's still with me. I have to believe that because it's what keeps me going."

Ghosts at the New Ross Castle

The paranormal activity on the property in New Ross known as the "castle" was first recorded by Joan Harris, who lived there in the 1970s and 1980s. According to current owners, Alessandra Nadudvari and Tim Loncarich, during the time Joan lived there, she uncovered a complex of stone walls in her backyard.

Alessandra writes, "She [Joan] was not satisfied with the official explanation that they were the remnants of a 19th-century smithy. Instead, she formulated her own theories. One of them involved Vikings who are known to have sailed to Canada between the 11th and 14th centuries. The other theory centred on the 17th-century Scots who were Stuart supporters and who were persecuted by Oliver Cromwell."

According to Alessandra, Joan conducted extensive excavations on her property, which revealed the foundation walls, several carved stones and small artifacts. She documented her findings with photographs and sketches, which can be seen in her book *A Castle in Nova Scotia*.

There is a chapter dedicated to ghosts, fairies, strange lights, and faces appearing on frosted windows.

"Joan was an intrepid explorer who was not afraid of ghosts. She only worried that they would try to interfere with or thwart her excavations." Alessandra writes. "She observed several ghosts near the stone walls and wrote that they had thrown rocks on a pile. The local Mi'kmaq advised her to encourage the good spirits to stay (which in turn would cause the bad spirits to leave). Joan also saw ghosts in the basement of the house. It was the one place where she felt uneasy. On the first floor of the house, she sometimes heard disembodied voices of men speaking in monologue or having a conversation."

Tim Loncarich and Alessandra Nadudvari, current owners of the New Ross property known as the Castle.

According to Alessandra, the majority of ghosts seemed to be benevolent, although Joan also describes a few "bad apples." There were poltergeists in the house, which had the ability to move objects, make them disappear and then reappear out of thin air. The poltergeists opened locked doors and created "cold spots" in the house. They would "wrap" themselves around lights and cause them to dim. A few people reported feeling physically ill when these poltergeists were around.

Joan had green thumbs, Alessandra says, and she loved being outside in her garden. She saw fairies, flickering lights, and "bluish streaks" in the air. Faces of fairies and cupids appeared on frosted windows in winter.

"She made sketches of them and included them in her book. These invisible creatures would leave small gifts for her, for example an amethyst pendant. They also took things from her, for example her wedding band. She asked for it to be returned but it never was."

Despite her valiant efforts, Alessandra writes that Joan failed to prove to the archaeological community that the site was of historical significance. She succeeded in creating a legend of a castle, which grew in size over the years. Before long, various people attributed the walls not only to Vikings and Scots, but also to Celts, Phoenicians, Templars, Henry Sinclair, and Acadians.

"Then the Templar treasure was inserted into the legend, which attracted the attention of treasure hunters intent on digging it up with brute force. When the property was put up for sale, my husband Tim and I purchased it [in 2015] with one goal — to protect it and to restore it, because it was in a sad shape."

Alessandra says they planned to use Joan's book as a guide to the backyard.

"There were photographs of the stone walls and sketches of carved stones, but no comprehensive map. We saw that the walls had been covered back up with dirt and were no longer visible to the naked eye, except for a section near the well. Moreover, provincial law prohibited any excavation without an archaeological permit, if the intent was to find historic artifacts. How could we see what was underground? Enter the psychics."

Alessandra explains that a group of paranormal investigators based in Liverpool contacted her and her husband with a generous offer to tour the property and to give it an intuitive inspection.

"We were curious because we had never seen a team of psychics before," she says. "They were accompanied by Mi'kmaw medium Shawn Leonard and artist Melissa Labrador. Shawn surprised us by bringing up the topic of Templars and Cathars. He said the people who had lived on the property were farmers. He suggested we hire a cadaver dog to identify potential graves, which we did not do, because it would further complicate the already complicated requirements of the law. The team dispersed on the property and turned on their recording devices in case there were ghosts who wanted to talk."

Alessandra recalls there seemed to be only one ghost present on that day.

"Melissa perceived that there was a spirit of a tall Frenchman standing in the trees in the boulder area. This was at the end of the property where, decades ago, the highway department had pushed some very large boulders onto a pile. Even Joan Harris did not know what lay underneath those boulders. If there was a place untouched and undisturbed by her excavations, it was here."

Alessandra says she and Tim asked Melissa to convey a message to the ghost, that they had friendly intentions and that they were not invaders.

"We also asked if there was something we could do for him — perform a favour or say a prayer. An answer came back that he missed the aroma of 'stinky cheese.' This elicited smiles all around. We made a plan to procure some stinky French cheese and bring it back the following day. We were able to find a loaf of Epoisses at Lunenburg farmers' market. We placed it at the foot of the tallest tree growing among the boulders. One of us (Alessandra) said the Lord's Prayer, thinking that the ghost might appreciate it. Surely, no one had prayed for his eternal peace in a long time."

This is the area at the back of the property where a spirit of a tall Frenchman has been seen standing in the trees in the boulder area. This is at the end of the property where, decades ago, the highway department had pushed some very large boulders onto a pile.

On another occasion, Alessandra says a visiting psychic from Ireland, Jackie Queally, dowsed the property.

"She used a pendant to identify some of the walls. We had an idea where they were, based on old photographs, but we did not tell her. Jackie walked confidently in a straight line right on top of them. She was drawn to the well and asked for permission to meditate there. She spent some time sitting on the lid with her eyes closed. When she came out of her meditative state, she described seeing a 'knight' in the well. It could have been an archetypal symbol rather than a real warrior, she said.

The knight was in motion and she demonstrated this by making a sharp, downward cut with her arm, like a warrior wielding a weapon."

Alessandra says the topic of ghosts and knights has been connected to the property now for many years.

"We became involved in the History Channel's docudrama *The Curse of Oak Island*. We met the brothers Rick and Marty Lagina, who led a major treasure hunt on Oak Island, which is only 20 kilometres south of New Ross. They heard that the same type of stone, which had used to line the fabled Money Pit, was on the bottom of our well. When the film crew came to visit us, they brought with them a diver who descended into the well. He found a mark on one of the stones, which resembled the British 'broad arrow.' To some people it looked more like a triangle or a pyramid with an eye."

Next, Alessandra says they showed them Herm, a standing stone, which had been unearthed by Joan.

"She found it lying face down and managed to raise it back up. She turned it so that it would face the well. Herm is a fascinating stone, which, according to dowsers, marks the spot of two crossing ley lines. One side of Herm, the one facing the well, is covered with a large cross, badly eroded by the elements. It bears a striking resemblance to the cross pattée; the signature symbol of the Order of the Knights Templar. We discussed this possibility with the film crew, although it was not the only explanation we had for the stone."

Alessandra says that due to publicity, she and Tim became increasingly worried about vandals who were bound to target Herm. A decision was made to move the stone to the safety of a museum and they reached an agreement with Queens County Museum, which offered to create an entire exhibit just for Herm.

"We were happy and excited," she says. "Many people wished to view the stone and it would be easier for them to do so in a museum, instead of having to track us down and arrange for a private tour. We discussed the logistics of transporting the heavy Herm with museum director Linda Rafuse. It was a conversation we had over the phone and no one else was privy to it. Or so we thought."

Alessandra says Linda called again the next day to report a rather strange incident.

"One of her employees had seen a ghost inside the museum. It was a tall man standing on the deck of the museum ship. His expression was stern and his gaze was directed at Linda's office. No one knew what it could mean. We asked Linda for a more detailed description of this spectral guest. The employee was kind enough to draw a rough sketch. We did not expect to see what she had drawn. It was a knight in armour. Was this our old friend from New Ross, the one with a taste for cheese? If he was, then we hoped he approved of the museum as a new home for Herm."

Alessandra says the last piece of strangeness occurred when *The Curse of Oak Island* film crew returned to New Ross in 2018 on a follow-up visit.

"Rick Lagina introduced us to a local resident who used to visit our property as a child. He and his cousin played there in the dirt with their Tonka trucks when they found a medallion. It was made of silver and its design matched that of a 17th-century medallion of the Order of the Garter. We saw photos of it," Alessandra says, adding there were French words on one side and the image of St. George slaying a dragon.

"The saint was portrayed as a knight on horseback with a long spear pointed down at the writhing dragon. We thought of Jackie Quealley and her perception that

This is the Herm Stone that Joan Harris found lying face down on her New Ross property. It can now be seen at the Queens County Museum in Liverpool.

a knight was somehow connected with the well and the property in general. She couldn't have known about the medallion, as the cousins had kept it under wraps for many years."

After a long and intense discussion about the significance of the silver medallion, the film crew packed up their gear and got ready to leave, she says.

"Tim went inside the house to see if they had forgotten any drink coolers or food in the kitchen. He found a small wooden cross on the table there. It was fashioned as a pendant, to be worn around the neck on a cord. Its left arm was longer than the right arm, just like the cross on the face of Herm stone. Tim asked every member of the crew if it belonged to him or her, but no one recognized it. We recalled how Joan Harris had received pendants as gifts from the invisible inhabitants of the house. But who was this gift for?"

Alessandra says Tim felt that the most deserving recipient was Rick Lagina, who accepted it graciously.

There's a Stranger in Our House

Dave and Rebecca bought what they thought was their dream home in the fall of 2005. Located on the rugged Atlantic coastline, the nearly 150-year-old house had everything the couple was looking for — three bedrooms, two bathrooms, a fully renovated kitchen and dining room area, and one and a half acres of land with a multi-million-dollar view.

"When we found this place, we literally thought we had hit the jackpot," Dave says. However, he quickly adds, "We should have realized that something wasn't right with the property when we learned that the home had been sitting on the market for nearly two years despite having been recently renovated and upgraded."

"That should have been our first clue that something wasn't right with this place," Rebecca adds. "But the real estate agent told us she felt the house was a little pricey and most people didn't see the value in the property, so it was just sitting there waiting for the right people to come along. I guess that was us. We fell in love with the place on the first visit and eventually we were able to negotiate with the owners and get the price down to a more reasonable level that we were willing to pay."

"We were extremely excited and happy with ourselves," Dave says. "We thought we had done a great thing in getting the sellers to come down to our terms but it wasn't long after we moved in that we found out that we had gotten more with this property than we had bargained for."

It's not that Dave and Rebecca are angry with the previous owners or the real estate agent for their lack of full disclosure, but no one had warned them that the house came with a spirit and not only that, it was an angry spirit.

"I always try to give people the benefit of the doubt so maybe they didn't know about the ghost," Rebecca says, "but I find it extremely hard to believe that the former owners didn't know what was going on in that house. And I honestly don't believe they should have sold it to us without fair warning. That just doesn't seem appropriate to me."

"Would we have still bought the place if we had known that it was haunted?" Dave asks. "I don't know but we should have been given a heads up. I had never been a real believer in that stuff before I moved in here, so who knows? We've talked about that over the years and it's more than likely that we would have still bought the place."

It wasn't long after the couple moved into the house in late September 2005 that things started going sideways.

"It was actually on the third day of being here that strange things started to happen," Rebecca says, explaining that she and her husband were in the kitchen unpacking boxes when they heard a ruckus on the second floor, where the bedrooms and one of the bathrooms are located. "It was just the two of us in the house and it was around 11 a.m. and it was warm for September. I remember it so vividly. Dave and I were putting dishes in the cupboards when all of a sudden we heard one of the doors to one of the bedrooms slam shut. … It scared the crap out of us."

"At first, I thought maybe it was the wind," Dave picks up the story. "The day before, we had had the windows open to air the place out because it had smelled a bit musty from being shut up for such a long time and so I thought maybe we had forgotten to close one of them."

"But then we heard another door slam shut and another and then another," Rebecca says. "And in between all of that, we could hear footsteps coming from the second floor. It was like someone was running from one room to the next slamming all the doors. It was so freaky and I admit I was scared. My first thought was that maybe someone had been squatting in the house before we bought it and they were still there and they were angry that we had moved in."

"Yeah, I'll admit it scared me too," Dave says. "I was convinced we weren't alone in the house and, actually, as we eventually found out, it turns out we weren't alone."

Dave says while he was intimidated by the noises coming from the second floor, he knew he had to check things out.

"What was I supposed to do? I had no choice but to go and see what was going on up there," he says, explaining that as he slowly made his way to the second floor, he told his wife she should be ready to get out of the house and call the police. "I had no idea what to expect to find when I got up there, but because of the commotion we had just heard, I really expected to find someone."

Cautiously opening each of the bedroom doors, Dave checked each room, including the closets, and inspected all the windows.

"I found nothing," he says, sounding almost disappointed. "The rooms were empty and all the windows on the second floor were closed and locked up tight. ... It was really unnerving." While he didn't really want to find a stranger lurking in his house, that would have been preferable to the alternative.

"We know what we heard," Rebecca says. "There was definitely someone or something, up there on our second floor that morning. After Dave came back downstairs and told me he hadn't found anything, my thoughts immediately went to the dark place."

"She immediately said, 'What if this place is haunted?'" Dave continues. "I didn't even want to think about that so I immediately shot her down. 'No way,' I said, and told her she was crazy for even thinking of that."

Today, however, Dave concedes his wife's first instincts were right on target.

"Those slamming doors and footsteps that we heard that morning were just the first of many strange things happening in our house," he says. "There are just so many incidents that have occurred over the years that it would be impossible to relate them all."

Rebecca says their emotions have run the gamut as their experiences have ranged from the casual slamming door and hearing footsteps while alone in the house, to seeing someone in a room with you, feeling someone touch you and throwing things around the room.

"I remember one night about a month after we moved in," she says, her voice cracking as she speaks. "I had gone to bed about an hour before Dave was supposed to come up. I was really tired and it didn't take me long to doze off, but I wasn't really in a deep sleep. You know what it's like when you're kind of half awake and half asleep, you are aware of things but still sort of in a daze.

That's the state I was in that night but I am 100 percent certain that I did not imagine what happened next."

About 15 minutes after she went to bed, Rebecca heard Dave come into the room and climb into bed with her.

"I heard him. I felt the bed move as he crawled in. I felt him next to me," Rebecca says. "But as I rolled around to ask him why he had come to bed so early I was shocked to find the bed empty." She pauses, takes a deep breath and continues, "I actually jumped out of bed, that's how freaked out I was."

"And I heard her scream," Dave says, explaining he was down in the living room watching a hockey game when he heard the commotion. "I knew something was wrong so I ran upstairs and when I got to the bedroom, I found her in a bad state. She was scared to death. Once I got her calmed down, I went downstairs and locked up all the doors and made sure everything was secure. After that, we went to bed, but neither of us slept well that night."

The couple have had more than their fair share of sleepless nights in the house, especially Rebecca, who says while she has never been comfortable staying alone in the house, she has had to deal with her fear and anxiety because Dave travels a lot for his job.

"There have been times when my panic has gotten the best of me and I've had to call a friend to come and stay with me or, on a few occasions, I've actually left the house and gone to stay with a friend. There were three of those incidents over the years."

The first time Rebecca fled the house was in the spring of 2006, less than a year after they had bought it.

"Dave was away for a couple of days on business and I was feeling especially nervous about being alone but on the second night, something happened that just scared me so badly, I had to leave," she says.

After making sure all the doors and windows were locked and secured, Rebecca went to bed around 10 p.m.

"When Dave's away, I don't sleep all that well, but it was really bad that night. I just felt like I wasn't alone. Truthfully, I had that kind of weird feeling all day. It was like someone was constantly watching me but I kept telling myself it was my imagination, that it was just my mind playing tricks on me — but it wasn't."

About an hour after going to bed, Rebecca says she was just lying there trying to force herself to go to sleep when she suddenly felt someone was hovering over the bed.

"You know how it is when you can sense that you are not alone? That's what it was like. I knew someone was there beside the bed and they were very close. I could feel them but I was afraid to open my eyes because I knew if I had opened my eyes and someone was looking back at me, I would have died right then and there. I was terrified because whatever it was it was very close to me and I really didn't want to see it."

She isn't sure how long she lay there, frozen with the covers pulled up to her nose, afraid to move or open her eyes, but she says it must have been at least 10 or 15 minutes.

"I was so scared," she recalls, the cracking in her voice betraying her emotions. "I honestly did not know what to do, but finally I told myself I had to open my eyes and face whatever was there. I couldn't stay like that all night. It was the worst feeling you could ever imagine."

Taking all the courage and strength she could muster, Rebecca slowly forced herself to open her eyes.

"I can tell you that I was never as afraid in my life as I was that night," she says. "I wished that Dave was there with me, but I was alone and I knew I had no other choice. But I can tell you, I don't know what I would have done if someone had been standing there. It was just the most frightening thing I had ever faced up to that point in my life."

She says she has no idea what was in her room that night, but when she opened her eyes whatever it was had disappeared.

"And I can tell you I was out of that room and out of that house as fast I could move," Rebecca says, adding that she didn't even stop to change her clothes. Instead, she just grabbed a coat and her purse on her way out the front door and drove to a friend's house where she spent the night.

"Dave was coming home the next day but I called him when I got to my friend's place and told him what had happened," she says. "The next day, when Dave got home, he went through the whole house from top to bottom and couldn't find anything. It freaks me out though because I would like to know why it only bothers me in the bedroom and not Dave."

While Dave has never had these types of experiences in the bedroom, he says he would never dismiss anything his wife tells him because he too has had his fair share of unexplained phenomena in the house.

"One afternoon, while I was watching a ballgame in the living room, I heard someone come in the back door, come through the kitchen and go up the stairs to the second floor," he says. "It was mid-afternoon and Becca had been in town with some friends for the morning so I thought it was her coming home. I yelled up and asked how things were going but when she didn't answer I went to the bottom of the stairs and yelled up again just in case something was wrong. I thought it might also be possible that maybe she hadn't heard me the first time."

Again, though, his wife didn't answer.

"But something did," he quickly continues, his demeanour stiffening as he speaks. "At this point, someone slammed the door to our bedroom and I thought something must be really wrong for Becca to do that instead of talking to me so I ran up the stairs and opened the bedroom door, expecting to find her there."

But the room was empty, he says.

"I swear to God, that this happened," he says. "It freaked me out so I quickly called Becca to see where she was and when she answered she told me she was still at her friend's place. I have to tell you that gave me cold chills right then and there. I have no idea who came in the house that day and went upstairs to our bedroom, but someone sure did."

Dave has had other encounters with whatever is haunting their house. On several occasions, he says someone touched him even though no one else was in the room with him.

"More than once, when I've fallen asleep while watching a hockey or ball game, someone has nudged me as if trying to get me to wake up," he explains. "I always think it's Becca telling me to turn off the television and go to bed if I'm going to sleep, but when I wake up, there's never anyone there and I usually find Becca fast sleep when I go to bed. That's more than a little unnerving."

Dave is a great cook and once, he recalls, while he was busy in the kitchen preparing a meal for some guests who were coming for dinner that evening, he says someone gently nudged him as they walked past.

"As I was working over a pot on the stove, I felt someone nudge me and I thought it was Becca wanting a taste," he says, with a grin. "She loves my honey and garlic chicken, which is what I was making for dinner that day, but when I turned around to tell her she'd have to wait for dinner, I realized I was alone in the kitchen."

"He actually called up to me in the bathroom to see if I had just been in the kitchen, but I was upstairs getting ready for our guests so it wasn't me," Rebecca says. "But we are used to that sort of thing by now. We get 'touched' all the time and we also hear voices as well, like someone talking."

"That is really strange when that happens," Dave says. "It's almost like a whisper and most of the time, while you can hear the voice, you can hardly decipher what they're saying. You have to listen really hard to figure out the words."

"Over the years, we've been able to figure out some of the things the voice is saying," Rebecca continues. "We're sure we've heard it say 'wagon' and 'brick' and 'window' and 'fire' and 'run fast' and, I think, 'basket.' And we've heard two names as well. We've heard it say 'Madelyn' and, we think it sounds like 'Whitehall' or 'Whiteheal.'"

"We have no idea what any of that means," Dave says. "It all just adds up to the mystery that surrounds this place, but we do know that the wife of one of the former owners, about 100 years ago, was named Madelyn. We often wondered if that meant anything."

While both Dave and Rebecca have had many experiences over the years, they have not been able to determine what these paranormal happenings could be related to.

"We've asked around with our neighbours and we've looked through old archives and newspaper records to try and find out if something tragic may have happened here, but we've had no luck," Rebecca says. "We would like to know what's going on so we've even had paranormal investigators and psychics come to the house to check things out, but that hasn't been very helpful. All they can tell us is that the house is shrouded in a dark energy. I say, no kidding. I could have told them that."

And even though they have lived in the house since 2005 and have had two children since moving there, they say they are still bothered by the spirit.

"It doesn't seem to happen as often these days," Dave says. "But it does still happen. It could be that we've just become more used to them and may not even notice when strange things happen."

"The kids have had experiences, too," Rebecca says. "But thankfully, not like the ones Dave and I have had. When they were young, they would ask if someone else lived in the house with us and we would assure them that nothing in this house would bother them. They seemed to accept things just fine and I don't ever recall either of them being so afraid that they weren't comfortable about being here."

"That's a good thing because if it would have been bothering the kids, we would have packed up and gotten the hell out of here," Dave says without hesitation. "But we're okay here. We've lived with this for a lot of years now and we don't feel threatened or intimidated in any way. It can sometimes be a little unnerving and even scary when something happens that you can't explain, but I don't think whatever is here wants to do us any harm. If so, it would have happened by now."

"We have talked about selling over the years," Rebecca admits. "But this is our home and we've just decided to treat our spirit as a guest. Am I happy that it's here? Absolutely not, but it seems like it's here to stay so we have just decided that we have to make the most it."

Author's note: The house described in the proceeding story is located somewhere in Nova Scotia. The owners have experienced such bizarre and strong paranormal occurrences that while they will agree to talk about them, they ask that their true identities be protected for fear of ridicule from non-believers. I have visited this location on several occasions and agreed to the couple's terms.

The Ghosts of Cross Island

It is a widely accepted fact that in the paranormal world some people are more in tune to the spiritual plane than others and some places seem to attract more paranormal activity than others.

Cross Island, a small wooded island that divides the approach to Lunenburg Bay into two channels, is one of those places.

Cross Island light is a white pyramidal tower, 11.7 m (38 feet) high on the east point of the island (44.19N 64.10W). A fog signal of two blasts every minute is sounded from a horn close to the light; the horn points 164 deg.

George Locke, originally from Cape Breton, made a career working at several lighthouses in Nova Scotia. His lighthouse-keeper career started with Flint Island near Cape Breton in 1975. It ended with Cross Island in July of 1989, when he and his family had to leave the newly automated lighthouse, as well as the island located near Lunenburg.

George and his family lived on Cross Island for nine years, while he worked there as a lightkeeper. He had previously worked as a fisherman and a skipper but ended up becoming a lightkeeper after his boat burned.

But he is quoted in an early CBC report as saying that he found his "niche" while living island life.

"It's a way of life, it's hard to explain, eh? You got to be part of it, I guess, to explain it," George told the CBC. "If you want to go for a walk, you can go for a walk. If you want to sit down and watch television, or if you want to read, you know, you're pretty well your own boss ... as long as you do your work and pick your own time to do it, nobody bothers you."

But George insisted that despite the isolation, he loved the job and loved working on the islands.

"We read a lot," he chuckled, but added that he and his family received many visitors on the island, particularly during the summer.

His wife told a newspaper about life on Cross Island, that she often served homemade bread and cookies to those who dropped by.

"We call it the Cross Island yacht club and our guest-book at the house is filled with names of friends who have visited us from all over the world," Ethel Locke said in a July 11, 1989 story that was printed on the other side of the country in the *Lethbridge Herald* about the closing of the lighthouse.

The Cross Island lighthouse had operated for more than a century and a half and until the Lockes left in July 1989, it had always had a lightkeeper living on the island.

In addition to the lighthouse and his family, George suspects that the island also had a few inhabitants of the paranormal persuasion.

"I didn't see anything personally," George says, when recalling his experiences on Cross Island. "But my son [Daniel] and wife [Ethel] surely did."

The Cross Island lighthouse had operated for more than a century and a half and until the Lockes left in July 1989 it had always had a lightkeeper living on the island. The place is also a hotbed of paranormal activity.

He tells the story of the day he and a family friend had gone to check the station boat on the north end of the island.

"And then I'll never forget the time the young fella ... I'll never forget that as long as I live."

He pauses and then picks up the story. "So anyway, we geared up and went down in the tractor, and when I come around the turn I thought I seen a light over in the harbour, eh? So I said to Daniel, 'Now Daniel [he was around 11 or 12 at the time],' I said, 'When we get down, I'll stop. You jump up, take the tractor back up the road to Oil Cove. Do it slow." And I said, "Me and Tom'll stay here and check the boat."

And that's what they did.

"So anyway, he went up the road. There was no light, no movement, no sound, so I said 'Tom, it couldn't have been. It must have been my imagination.' And I heard the tractor turn around at the top of Oil Cove Hill and come down over the hill, into the cove."

He pauses again. Then tells the story:

And then, I heard this ungodly scream. And the tractor started wide open. And he comes down over that road as fast as that tractor could go and he was just a-screamin'. He was terrified! When I got him calmed down, I said, 'What in the hell is wrong?'

He said 'Dad, there's a man standin' in the middle of the road,' he said, 'and he scared me and I run him down!'

I said, 'What?'

He said, 'There was a man ...'

"Go on," I said, 'There's no way there's anybody on this island!'

'Dad,' he said, 'I seen him!' He said, 'He was standin' in the middle of the road and I run him down!'

'Well,' I said. 'Come on and let's go back and look.' [My friend] Tom was a superstitious man. He was terrified of ghosts and stuff like that, Tom was. So I said. 'C'mon Tom, let's go up.' So I went up and I said, 'Where was he?'

Daniel said, 'He was right there! Look! He was right there, Dad. I'm tellin' you he was right there!'

Dan explained to his father that he had come back down to the road and stopped where the woods meet on both sides. When he did, he looked up and there was a man standing in front of him.

All he could see of the man was from his waist up over the engine bonnet of the tractor but he was glowing white. The man was wearing a fishermen's knit sweater and Dan could still see the wool in his shirt. "And he had them hats that go on the side, an old Irish hat, you know what I mean? Tam or whatever they're called. And he scared the shit out of me and I ran over him!"

Describing the man, Dan said he had a greyish-brownish beard.

"I remember that. He had chubby cheeks. I remember same as it was yesterday. Friendly-lookin' guy. Looked like a, I don't know, an old Irish kind of dude or somethin' like that, right? Just happened fast, eh? He was just standin' there. He had his head cocked to one side a little bit, hat on. Couldn't see no arms or nuttin' like that. They must have been down by his side."

George continues the story:

So I got out [with a] flashlight. It was after rainin' that day, but there was no tracks in the mud, no tracks there, so I got thrashing through the woods, to look and see if there were anybody.

Tom said, 'There's no goddamn way you'd get me go in that woods!'

So anyway, I said, 'Dan, it's your imagination. It was a stump or something. You thought it was in the middle of the road.'

I pass it off like that.

So anyway, Smitty (a former lightkeeper on the island) come down that weekend. And Dan started to talk about it. And Smitty said, 'What'd he look like?' And when Dan described what he looked like — it was an old man with a beard and a turtleneck sweater — and right away, Smitty named him.

And Daniel said, 'Did he die on the island?'

'No,' Smitty said. 'He didn't die on the island, but he was a lightkeeper here for about 20 years. But he's dead now.'

When asked what year this happened, George says, "Went there in '80. I'd say about '85. '84, '85, p'raps '86, around that, eh? Dan would know. He'll never forget that. You know what I mean. He seen ... far as I'm concerned, he seen it. He described that man and Smitty could tell who it was, so he seen something, eh."

Furthermore, George says, whatever his son saw that night scared him so badly that it was years before he would go back to that area at night.

George Locke and his family lived on Cross Island for nine years, while he worked there as a lightkeeper.

But George says his son wasn't the only person who experienced "strange things" on Cross Island. His late wife, Ethel, also had her run-ins with the island spirits. She also had a special connection to the island, he says.

George recalls one day when he and Daniel were over on the slip working on the boat and he saw Ethel walking down the road.

"The tractor was all smashed up then and wasn't working," he explains. "So I told Daniel to go over and pick up his mother at the landing. So Dan jumped in the punt and on the way over he stopped and hauled a lobster trap and went over and picked up his mother. She said to him, 'How much fish did Smitty have today?' but Dan told her he wasn't talking to Smitty."

George recalls his wife was ready to argue.

"She said, 'Don't tell me you wasn't talkin' to Smitty. I just watched you.'"

She wouldn't believe Dan even though he tried to tell her many times he hadn't been talking to Smitty.

"So you know her. She went over to the slip then and she asked me about Smitty and I told her that I wasn't talking to Smitty that day. 'We never seen him,' I told her."

George says he isn't sure whether or not Smitty steamed up the harbour then.

"But we went up to Smitty's camp for supper that night and Ethel said, 'Talkin' to Daniel today, Smitty?' He said, 'No, it's the first time I seen Daniel today.' Ethel explained what it looked like, the boat. 'Holy Jesus! There's Jim,' Smitty said. 'Welcome to Cross Island!'"

Jim Burgoyne was supposed to be a lobster fisherman who lived on the island years before George and family moved there.

"They say he was supposed to have drowned on The Hounds, that's all I know about him," George says, adding that was just one of the many times that Ethel said she saw someone when there wasn't anyone there.

As for George himself, he says he never experienced any of that "strange stuff" on Cross Island, but he agrees it was an unusual place.

"Just living on a small island like that was a different way of life, as it is," George says. "But when you got all this other kind of weird stuff going that makes it even more interesting."

Strange but True

The Ghost Ship of Summerville Beach

There is a beautiful beach located on the South Shore of Nova Scotia where, according to local legend, every seven years the wreckage of a mysterious vessel shows itself to curiosity seekers.

Known as the Ghost Ship of Summerville Beach (in the Region of Queens) it is believed the pieces of the wooden vessel have been buried under the shifting sands for several centuries as they have been noted in local historical documents down through the years including the famous diaries of early Liverpool settler and Privateer Simeon Perkins.

Today, the Perkins Diaries are considered the definitive historical record of colonial settlement in Nova Scotia. Several passages in Perkins' diary (1766-1780) may hold the secret of the Ghost Ship of Summerville Beach.

On September 20, 1778, Perkins recorded, "There was an engagement between a Halifax cruiser — (perhaps TRUBLU) — and a privateer sloop from Dartmouth (probably Dartmouth, Mass.) at Port Mouton. The sloop ran near the shore, brought her guns to bear on the ship to keep off the enemy."

The next diary entry concerning shipping made by Perkins on September 24,1778, was: "It was recorded that the privateer burned their vessel and saved the guns."

But a more probable solution is this October 25, 1778 dairy entry: "Mr. Hallett Collins reported a ship and sloop came into Port Mutton. The privateer sloop ran ashore and they set fire to her themselves. The schooner went out."

While it is possible that one of the vessels Perkins refers to in his diary is the one that rests below the shifting sands of Summerville Beach, the truth is that no one really knows anything for sure about the mysterious wreckage. However, there are lots of theories about its identity, including the possibility that it could be the remains of an early Viking vessel or a Spanish galleon that once sailed in the waters off what is now the province of Nova Scotia or a Privateer vessel that patrolled the troubled waters of the North Atlantic.

Historical records show that many vessels met their demise off Little Hope Island, located just off Port Joli Point. It is highly possible that wreckage from any one of these ships could have floated down the coast into Port Mouton Bay and come to rest onto Summerville Beach.

Over the decades, visitors to Summerville Beach have observed several pieces of oak planks in the sand at low water, near Broad River at the far end of the beach. The planks are secured to members just below the surface by wooden pins at each joint. These planks were visible again during several weeks in July 2018.

According to local legend, every seven years the wreckage of a mysterious vessel on Summerville Beach shows itself to the curiosity seekers. These images were taken in the summer of 2018 when the wreckage was visible for about two weeks.

One local researcher with a piqued interest in the Summerville Beach wreckage, David Pottier, shares his theory of the mysterious vessel that comes and goes with the shifting sands.

"The wooden wreck has been on the beach all of our lives," he says, noting that local lore says that the ship may reappear about every seven years before vanishing into the sands once more.

The summer of 2018 saw her return and Pottier says not having seen her in 40 years, he felt locals needed to protect the wreck and try to learn where she was built and her age.

These are the facts, he says — she was built from solid oak, stitched together with wooden treenails. American naval vessels were oak but there are no records of such a wreck in these waters. Bronze nails came into use around 1553. A metal detector found nothing — no metal — so the wreck is older, possibly much older, than the 16th century.

"An Israeli friend of mine, both Naval architect and archaeologist, gave me a direction about what to look for. He was right, our wreck matched 16th-century French naval specifications. Champlain arrived in Port Mouton Bay in 1604 but there are no records of a lost naval vessel since then."

The exposed oak keel, not reported previously, had the letter Y carved by the final dovetail. Working towards the bow, 25 letters X distance to next exposed dovetail, the local wreck had a keel length over 60 feet long.

"From the letter 'Y' carved into the keel, the exposed structure we are familiar with is the stern castle, which is in a capsized position."

What could the ghost ship have been, Pottier wonders? Where did she come from? Pottier has a theory.

"Spanish Galleons were known to have transited and sunk in our waters in the early 17th century, but bronze nails were used to set their treenails, so that can't be it," he explains. "She could be Basque, whose fishery existed off Newfoundland as early as 1525, but there are no records of Basque whaling in this area. The Basque fishery ended in 1625."

The Basque whaling industry in North America lasted from 1525 until 1625. To date, the oldest shipwreck ever discovered in Canadian waters is the Basque whaling galleon *San Juan*, which sank near the shore of Red Bay, Labrador in the autumn of 1565. The *San Juan* was a 52-foot, three-masted, 250-ton ship.

Pottier says the marine archaeologist who retrieved the whaler *San Juan* told him she was built using bronze nails.

"This fits within what we know about this period in ship-building. Nails came into use in 1553. The Summerville wreck has been scanned with a metal detector and has no nails."

Or, he continues, "She could also be part of the lost Knights Templar treasure fleet that sailed from La Rochelle, France and vanished. Today, clues to the Templar fleet's final destination all point to Oak Island."

Our ghost ship needs to be aged, identified and preserved. It is our heritage, he says, adding that until definitive research is complete, the mystery of the Summerville Ghost Ship will remain.

Tales from the Gravekeeper

Good evening.

My name is Jerome the Gravekeeper, and for centuries I've been looking after a couple of cemeteries in the most historically rich, amazing area in all of North America. The intriguing tales formulating from the fascinating locals help to form the backbone of our haunted Annapolis Valley.

I was first employed in 1763, so I've known a lot of people who have come and gone from our magnetically gorgeous neck of the woods. So many people in fact that, unless you have a prearranged reservation, both hallowed grounds are no longer accepting new arrivals. Needless to say, it's not as busy as it once was in Wolfville's Old Burial Grounds or Kentville's Oak Grove Cemetery. I assure you though, the memories remain.

Not only are these grounds stunning — you're welcome — but they continue to demonstrate historical facts. The sandstone markers have worn faster than those of granite and marble, so it's reassuring to know that detailed accounts have been recorded throughout the decades. We've documented our dead very well 'round here and it's an absolute pleasure to honour those long passed.

Some of us died tragically, while others contributed for many years. Regardless of the durations of our lives, we've all had our chances to impact our surrounding communities. To help pass the time, 12 years ago my ghostly friends and I created a way to share our vast cultural riches. We've got things figured out by now, but at first things weren't so clear.

I have a friend an hour away, at the Southwestern end of the Valley, named Alan Melanson. He's not ghostly, but he can trace his Acadian ancestry back 10 generations. When he speaks of the Melanson Settlement National Historic Site across the river, he's talking about his own flesh and blood. For close to 30 years he's been conducting award-winning Candlelight Graveyard Tours at Fort Anne in Annapolis Royal. If you end up catching him in action, please pass on Jerome the Gravekeeper's greetings. You'll be inspired by his knowledge and his passion, probably just like I was almost 13 years ago.

Photos by Andrea Burbidge

Jerome the Gravekeeper (a.k.a. Jeremy Novak) shares stories from beyond the grave.

With his encouragement, the idea for Valley Ghost Walks was summoned and I knew I was going to have to lead it. Although I understood the overall concept, the content was murky. Were they to be historic? Or more paranormal? We have both options. What mix of the two was to become the winning formula? What was I most comfortable with?

I believe that there's realms out there we can't normally experience, so I've never intended to play around with things too too much. Someone suggested asking Edna Aker in Kentville for her take on the Ghost Walks idea. I now know that booking an appointment with this popular local psychic is required, but she was gracious enough to offer some sagely advice in her magical lobby after we showed up unannounced.

No, she wasn't interested in coming into the cemeteries to tell us where the "hotspots" were. Instead she countered, in a completely serious tone, and warned us to never go into a cemetery after drinking or altering the mind. You see, hitchhikers use opened doors as a way out and it is best not to risk taking any uninvited guests home. With her encouragement, I knew respect was paramount when treading over those long ago passed. Valley Ghost Walks were to be family-friendly and more historical than anything else.

Word must have spread quickly because we were approached by John Hebert, a psychic from Kingston, Ontario, at the beginning of our second year. It's well documented that Seminary House on Acadia University's campus is haunted; we regularly share what is recorded on our walks. John was interested in knowing more about the haunting of Seminary, so I called on those I figured could help, and that summer, after the students had vacated, nine of us gathered at the site. Oonagh had a master key.

Seminary stories have been told to freshmen for decades. Go ahead, ask to see the file in the Acadia archive room below the library. Opened in 1879, Seminary

House is the oldest building on any Nova Scotia university soil. Many rooms have recorded strange occurrences.

The story that gets the most attention is that of Constance Hagan. Legend says she was a nursing student who became pregnant out of wedlock and that her name no longer appears in Acadia University's record books. Scared and alone while attending a strict Baptist university, she took her own life by hanging between the third and fourth floors from the "banistered well," an opening in the floor used to let light pass. As we made it up to the top floor with our group, it was clear that this gap had been filled in many years ago.

With little fanfare, we visited the rooms that had had verified sightings. One of them doesn't exist anymore. It's been turned into an elevator. My memory is shady so I'm not 100 percent certain, but I believe we were walking by room 427 when John expressed a desire to enter. Because of his mumbling, it was hard to understand every word he had to say, but we did watch intensely from the doorway.

John stood in silence. After a short time, his eyes rolled back and he stumbled. In fact, he almost fell over. Thankfully he recovered quickly and was able to exit on his own accord, as I had no intention of entering. Of course we were all very curious to know what he had just experienced.

To the best of our ability to understand him, John told us that bad things have happened in that room. He didn't elaborate any further than recalling three girls playing a Ouija board and being tied up. We were all too spooked to ask him any follow-up questions. Needless to say, this odd happening has become excellent content. I've been telling these details on Wolfville's Gravely Ghost Walk for years, but only once have I heard a gasp from an audience member, a young woman. I asked her what was so upsetting and she replied, "That's my room!" I'm glad I'm not staying in Seminary tonight.

Later, I took John to the corner of Highland Avenue and Main Street. At that time there still stood a little blue house just off the corner. There's a photo in Tom Sheppard's great historic Wolfville book that shows the Porter's Brothers Store, in which you can just barely see the alleyway between the buildings.

It was in this alley where Bessie Harris was said to have been murdered by her separated husband, Albert DeWolf, in 1879. She's been telling her unfortunate tale on our walks since day one, so I wanted to test John. I asked him to walk down the eastern tree-lined driveway, but I didn't explain any more detail than that. After some time, he walked back to the sidewalk and stammered how something didn't feel quite right back in the deep, dark corner. He felt that there was probably a lover's quarrel many years ago. Well, that level of precision lends more credibility to his claim that there used to be a body buried to the west of the path, just in front of the Old Burial Ground's central circle, but no longer.

It's well documented that the prominent Baptist minister Edward Veery was disinterred and brought back to New Brunswick just six months after drowning in the Minas Basin boating disaster alongside Dr. Issac Chipman and four graduating students in 1852. You might argue that Jerome ought to be able recall the exact location of this disinterment, but I was on sabbatical in St. Augustine, Florida in 1852. As wonderful as this town is, it's good to get out every now and again. I've never claimed to have been the hardest working gravekeeper.

Today is our turn to uncover and share our past, but tomorrow it will be a responsibility for someone else.

We never know how much time we have to do the things we have been placed here to do. Inspiration comes from many places, and I pray that your light will continue to burn as brightly as possible as you face your own personal darknesses.

The surrounding community resources are vast in this valley, and it's been a special place for many, many generations. Just ask the Mi'kmaq.